M000033298

Rich

Relationships

Our Marital
Code to Oneness

Gilbert And Renée Beavers

Copyright © 2020 Gil & Renée Beavers.

Scripture taken from The Holy Bible, NEW INTERNATIONAL VERSION®. Copyright © 1973, 1978, 1984, 2011 by Biblica, Inc. All rights reserved worldwide. Used by permission. NEW INTERNATIONAL VERSION® and NIV® are registered trademarks of Biblica, Inc. Use of either trademark for the offering of goods or services requires the prior written consent of Biblica US, Inc.

This book is a work of non-fiction. Unless otherwise noted, the author and the publisher make no explicit guarantees as to the accuracy of the information contained in this book, and in some cases, names of people and places have been altered to protect their privacy.

All rights reserved. No part of this book may be used or reproduced by any means, graphic, electronic, or mechanical, including photocopying, recording, taping or by any information storage retrieval system without the written permission of the author except in the case of brief quotations embodied in critical articles and reviews.

Because of the dynamic nature of the Internet, any web addresses or links contained in this book may have changed since publication and may no longer be valid. The views expressed in this work are solely those of the author and do not necessarily reflect the views of the publisher, and the publisher hereby disclaims any responsibility for them.

Any person depicted in stock imagery provided by Thinkstock are models, and such images are being used for illustrative purposes only.

Rich Book Business Coaching

www.richrelationshipsus.com.

ISBN: 978-1-7357018-5-1-Paperback

Foreword

BISHOP GEOFFREY V. DUDLEY, SR., PH.D., D.MIN.

God provided marriage and family as a fundamental building block for society and the propagation of the kingdom. He entrusted Jesus, the Savior of the world, in the hands of Mary and Joseph's marriage. God was up to something when he designed marriage and entrusted humanity with it.

Despite society and the Supreme Court rulings tinkering with marriage, it is still God's idea. Marriage is a mix of ups and downs, laughter and tears, joy and pain, covenant and crisis, romance and routine, victories and defeat. Adam and Eve gave us the first example of marriage as noted in Genesis 2:23-24, the New International Version, "... bone of my bone and flesh of my flesh... the two became one." However, their missteps have caused all marriages to watch their steps. Now, we have the Word as a lamp unto our pathway to overcome the errors of Adam and Eve. While the Word is the absolute guide to a successful marriage, the syncretization and application of the Word is also needed. Rich Relationships Podcast and "Our Marital Code to Oneness" are marriage guidance and principles at its best.

Gil and Renée capture all those moments to empower your marriage with their book. Their journey becomes a road map to having a successful marriage with a variety of real-life couple's stories as mile markers along the way. They compassionately and skillfully articulate how to win in your marriage. They employ their experience in this seminal work. It is filled with easy to follow steps to a better marriage. First Lady and I count them as one of the couples in the country we watch as inspiring influencers in the marriage enrichment space. Read this book and let it inform your efforts to build the ecosystem that will nurture your marriage to what God designed it to be.

Bishop Geoffrey V. Dudley, Sr., Ph.D., D.Min.

Bishop Dudley is the founding pastor of New Life in Christ Church in O'Fallon, IL, where he and First Lady Glenda serve not only their church, but the surrounding Metro East community. He is releasing his next book, "Family'ish: How to Raise a Fabulous Family," this year. It will be connected to his learning management system and podcast on www.ileadacademy.net where he is equipping leaders and emerging leaders in all aspects from home, to church, to community, and more importantly, self. iLead in Any Room Podcast can be found there and wherever you listen to podcasts!

Dedication

We are dedicating this book to the Institution of Marriage. Some of us still believe in YOU!

Our Relationship With Change: Renée M. Beavers.

I am Renée M. Beavers, a fifty-two-year-old woman, and my hometown is Detroit, Michigan. We are a retired Air Force family who has lived in thirteen cities in the US and overseas. I have to turn my back from the mundane and what made me comfortable in order to embrace the unfamiliar to grow. I had to become comfortable being uncomfortable. I have experienced different cultures, traditions, and people in my lifetime. I loved growing up in a big city. I have lived in small towns, as well. While living in a big city can make you open to new people, ideas, and cultures, I love the closeness I observed in small towns, the traditions, and lifelong relationships. Living in a small town can make you closed-minded to new people and experiences. There has to be a balance between remaining open to change while maintaining a commitment to your core values and healthy relationships. Living our lives with grace for differences, makes us kind, and ensures we will continue to improve and mature.

I am choosing to give myself permission to live well and overcome vitiligo, celiac disease, and osteoarthritis. Making food my medicine was my bravest moment. Pain, sickness, and medical conditions can get our attention, unlike anything else. I gave up my twenty-eight-year career as a Salon Owner & Hair Care Professional to become an author, speaker, and food evangelist. Living daily with food as a medicine and not a prescription drug, was my wisest decision. My commitment to change my life has positioned me to lead others on a journey of learning the power of food as medicine. This choice has taught me that life is a journey, not a destination, or an event. We are growing and changing; becoming the person God created us to become, one decision, and sometimes, one career at a time.

Being a woman has held me back, because I am called into a man's world. Public speaking and Evangelism are positions usually held by men. Even getting the help needed from my doctors was affected by my being a woman. Some of my medical professionals overlooked my symptoms. Sometimes women are not taken as seriously as men when they make medical claims.

While these obvious barriers have made things difficult, they have also strengthened me. It's forced me to study harder, gather more evidence-based data, and it has motivated me to create a solution-based program. I love being a woman. I know I am unique and one of a kind!

The greatest strength any woman can possess is the power to know and love the reflection in the mirror from the inside out. The love I have for myself permeates my relationships. My life is full! The two men whose support and love mean the most, have put their seal in my heart and mind. Thank you, Abba God and Gil, you are my everything. That love empowered me to love, nurture, and care for others. I am created for greatness, and with that same knowledge, I am empowered, and I empower and lift others up.

If I had to summarize my life in one dream, it would be that my life would make a difference forever and into eternity; and, that I would not only be successful in relationships, but also with God's resources. Becoming an author is a lifelong dream I didn't realize I had. As an author, I will accomplish my life dream. Writing books makes you eternal, it has realized my lifelong dream. My life and all the people and the events of my life will live on forever in my books, providing love, hope, freedom, and liberty to its readers.

This will come as a shock to people that don't know me, and it will be painful for the people who do. Nonetheless, it's my truth. Two selfish people who were addicted to drugs raised me. I had to grow up fast, and I was a parent to my young siblings. Not only did I proclaim and profess that I would never have children. I didn't even like people who had children. I talk about living a life with fewer regrets. If I had to say what my biggest regret is, it would be that I allowed the death of my beloved godmother to make me lie to myself about who I was and who I was not. Her belief was every woman should leave their mark on the world by having a child.

I didn't share this belief, but her death made me act as if I did. The girl who hated her mom, would now become a mother, how sad? No, I do not regret our daughter! I regret why and when we had her. I now know what you do is not as important as when and why you do it. Yes, all things work for Good for those who love God. It doesn't erase the consequences, and I must unpack each choice I make. I was twenty-one when we got married and twenty-three when we had our daughter. I know now, you can never be too old or too young for a task, but you can be too hurt.

My decision to have a child was not from my deep love and adoration for my amazing husband. It was from the deep hurt and loss of my godmother. She did not give birth to me, but she imparted life into my being. I didn't know at twenty-three what I know today. Before our daughter would reach ten months old, a serial killer took my mother's life. My stepfather died of cancer, my twenty-three-year-old husband and I faced the decision to adopt my then nine- and ten-year-old sisters. Again, the decision to parent was paired with pain, hurt, and death. Unfortunately, we committed a betrayal against ourselves and adopted two girls. Yes, they were my flesh and blood, but strangers, nonetheless.

I moved away from home when I was eighteen and got married when I was twenty-one. My husband and I were the people who sent nice gifts for birthdays and Christmas; we were not their parents. The decision for when and why to become a parent is my biggest regret. Unfortunately, I would say parenting has and still is my most significant area of growth. Our decisions must be ours. We must choose our why and commit to our why.

Are you happy? Happy means everything is going as planned. By that definition, I have never been or will never be happy. In my life, things don't go as planned. I have allowed Joy to fuel and govern my life. I am overwhelmed with joy each day. I am an overachiever; I love processes, order, and results. I have to remind myself daily that the process of life is the journey, and without the process, I would not have established the stamina to thrive once I reach a destination. In life, there are different destinations for different stages in life.

I married my best friend and learned to be a good listener and practice what I heard. Love is a choice; it makes our life and relationships count. Building something that didn't exist, for something you have never seen, for people who don't want it, is challenging. Having this same assignment, taking years to grow, can become discouraging. This is what the Freedom from Food program is. I am new to the roles of Author, Speaker, and Teacher, and so is my Relationship Lifestyle Movement. I want to fight for people's healthy relationships, not fight with them about it. My daily challenge is not whether to quit every day, but should I begin each day again? I am a Plant-Based Food Evangelists & Relationships Lifestyle Strategist. I spark awareness, encourage taking responsibility, and I empower individuals to make choices that support healthy choices and relationships. I love God and people.

Who, How, Why?

The answer to these three questions can make or break us. Today, I am a Christ-follower! I am a wife, mother, sister, friend, entrepreneur, author, and lifestyle strategist. With so many titles as women, we must discover our why. After owning and building salons for twenty-eight years, I have realized that I found my identity not in my God-given purpose, but in my ability to generate income. Living your life motivated by "How" and money is exhausting in our information-driven societies. There are millions of how-to-have ideas. Most of them will produce results. Yet, "How" without "Why" is like a day without night! It is out of balance, and it will wear you out.

I know who I am! Learning "How" to achieve a task or goal is also somewhat easy to do, if we don't take the long journey inward to discover our "Why." "Who" will rule our lives and crowd out our intimacy with God, ourselves, and others? I loved doing hair, and I was good at it; and yes, I made a lot of money. If you asked me during that time about my life, I would have shared that I was living "My Best Life." The keyword is I was living 'my' best life! Not for God, but for me and mine only. Being comfortable can be so dangerous. In our comfort, we are not dependent on hearing God or even asking Him for our next step.

I would always brag and say I could do hair with my eyes closed! That's a very dangerous place to remain. We grow when we are stretched, challenged, and uncomfortable. My books, website, social media, group, and individual sessions are how we share our results-based solutions. I am driven to learn lessons and lead myself and others into true life change with fewer regrets. Obstacles strengthen us, and they are as valuable as our opportunities. My biggest obstacle in life is failing to get to the root of my obstacles and my pain. God will call each of His children out into the deep, off the sidelines, and yes, to do something that makes us feel uncomfortable. Life is unfair. We will all have horrible, tragic things that will happen in our lifetime, and they will hurt us. What we do with our hurt differentiates and defines us. Yeah, there's always pain and difficulty knitted into our good news. It makes us sober and grateful.

Today, I am becoming the woman God designed me to become; the things that scared me to death, are now a part of my daily life. I write books, speak in front of large, small, and one-on-one groups. I speak on radio and television. My husband and I host a weekly podcast, have a relationship mobile app, and we mentor couples via Zoom weekly. Yes, this once very insecure, overweight girl, with low self-esteem, is now thriving in an environment where she was born to belong. Although, I must admit that I would have never picked this life for myself. From writing four books, sending out hundreds of press releases, holding radio interviews in my closet (to achieve excellent sound quality), and being told 'no' thousands of times, I can say with certainty, that this is what I was created for.

If I have learned only one lesson worth sharing, it is the power of unpacking your "Why" before you invest in your how, which will save you and others priceless time. Why do I wake up each day not knowing the outcome, but still have hope and joy each day? My "Why" is God loves me and He loves everyone around me, even the people I didn't know or like. God wants to use my mess, my pain, and my failures. All I have to do is willingly give them to Him, and He turns them into something beautiful. I hope my living God's life in the power of my unpacked "Why", encourages you to discover your why. What do I mean by unpacked? I will give you an example. For years, I lost and gained weight, had unresolved conflicts with people, and did not know how to use my voice for good. I had to ask myself, "Why?" What is the common thread in these seemingly different events? Me, it's me! I cannot control anyone or anything around me. My "Why" is for me? Why don't I use my power and energy to change me? Why don't I set boundaries, limits, and have realistic expectations for myself and others? "Why" don't I learn to say 'no' to myself and others? "Why" have I wasted so much time? "Why" can't I forgive? "Why" can't I ask for forgiveness? I asked myself, "Why?" until there were no whys left. I call this unpacking yourself. Our "Why" is the key to finding peace and solutions?

Today, I charge you to use your choices in ways that serve you well and empower you to develop the strength to serve God and others. That is the success that brings hope, freedom, and liberty. We can't pick our families of origin, our DNA, or even our facial features. We can control our time, our choices, and our habits. Examine them, manage them, and we must own them! Remember, we are more alike than we are different. You are not alone! Your story, your pain, and your difficulty are not unique. However, you are! And there is more to life than living for yourself, alone.

Take the journey inward to get to know and love God, yourself, and others. Know and love your family and others. Be kind to yourself and others. Have dreams that are so big that they rattle your mind, causing you to need the help of others to accomplish them. Own and unpack your "Why." Know and trust that God has a good plan for your life filled with love, laughter, pain, disappointment, and purpose.

I am an "Unstoppable, Woman in Christ Jesus." My name is Renée M. Beavers, and to look at me on the outside, I appear to be just like everyone else, and I am like you. I like to stay honest, open, and transparent (H.O.T.); it is how I thrive in relationships. You and I are more alike than we are different. If you asked how I became the person I am today, I would say I am a product of my choices, and not just my environment alone. Our choices form our habits, and our habits shape our lifestyles. Many of us have had our share of disappointment, sadness, heartbreak, and childhood of origin issues, rejection, betrayal, failure, and sickness. The five-million-dollar question is, "What will we do with it?" Do we unpack it, or do we act as if we're OK? The choice is ours to make, but the effects impact everyone. We have the same basic needs. Love, belonging, security, and purpose connects us to one another and God. Let's unpack the pain of our past together. It weighs us down!

Our Marital Code to Oneness:
Gil & Renée Beavers

We are the hosts of the Rich Relationships Podcast. This is our first anthologist experience. Gil and I are learning, growing, and enjoying the journey. The Rich Relationships Marital Code to Oneness is an anthology with seventeen powerful couples and two subject matter experts. With our more than thirty-year marriage and fifteen-year experience with engaged and married couples, it is the catalyst for the Rich Relationships project. Marriage is one of the most overlooked and underserved areas of ministry in most churches. We will bridge the gap between engagement and marriage. The Rich Relationships "Our Marital CODE to Oneness is more than a book, it's a community. Rich Relationships Our Marital Code to Oneness will provide examples of how to apply biblical principles to our marriage and relationships.

Gil and I have owned and sold multiple homes. We are blessed beyond measure! Building a home from beginning to end is a dream for many couples. We can put a check in that box; we have experienced building a house from the ground up as well. This process was probably the most meaningful of our homeownership experiences. Watching the process was remarkable and life-changing.

New homes and marriages have a lot more in common than we ever realized. Building a home has far more steps than marriage, so to keep it simple, we will not go through every step of the home building process. We will only focus on three. The Foundation, The Framework, and The Code. The Foundation is what our marriage is built on, Love or Fear. What we build our marriage on is our choice, let's get to work, together.

Love Gil & Renée Beavers

Working on your Marriage:
Gil & Renée Beavers

What is the difference between working *in* your marriage and working *on* your marriage? By design, the marriage relationship requires three to become "one," God, you, and your spouse. Personal inventory of our heart is one of the most neglected disciplines for most individuals. We need to develop our relationship with God by reading the Bible, praying, and daily worship. The journey inward is the longest and most neglected journey, but why?

Looking for growth areas in others is natural and comfortable. When will we ask ourselves the hard questions like, "Who am I? Who told me that? Who hurt you?" Relationships are where we have the highest likelihood to grow, if we are willing to do the work. We have to unpack and examine ourselves. Working *in* your marriage begins with looking at the reflection in the mirror, while working *on* our marriage, requires developing the necessary tools to make a healthy relationship our reality. Yes, healthy relationships require work, and that work begins with us.

Living for love is the only way to truly thrive in our marriage. After doing hair and owning salons for twenty-eight years, you get to meet hundreds of women who openly share their stories with you. As I look back, my career was like a never-ending case study. I believe being a good listener saves time and emotional energy. When someone shares their story with you, and you hear and see the results of unhealthy relationships, your heart grieves with the person that is sharing. After years of women sharing the same old story, I began to pray that God could use what I was told in order to help others learn to have better views and tools in relationships with God, themselves, and others.

The Bible is a living love letter filled with hope, principles, directions, and solutions. Nowadays, most people do not have a knowledge problem; we have an application problem. We need to be taught to see ourselves the way God does! We are more than enough, and we are complete in Him. Why is this important? How we view God and ourselves shape and determine what we look for in relationships. Someone who has a source cannot be our source. We should not seek to find our value and identity externally. Why do I say that? Many of us believe that getting married is the answer to our deepest unmet needs, and it is not. Jesus is! We were created as the object of God's affection, not for another person. When this is our view, we take the weight of our fulfillment off another human being's shoulders. Marriage is where we learn to become selfless and serve God and our mates. Marriage is spiritual warfare, not a romantic balcony alone.

Our marriage is our gift to God, each other, and the world. Getting empty is crucial to having healthy, Rich Relationships. When we unpack our wrong view of marriage, our uncommunicated thoughts, and our expectations, we are letting go of the pain, shame, and disappointment from our past. We are then making room for all the incredible blessings designed to fill our lives when we have Christ-centered marriages. Hopefully, we understand why working *in* our marriage has to take place before working *on* our marriage. Today, look at your views on relationships, listen to your pain, forgive yourself, and others. Hopefully, you are ready to move forward towards healthy, Rich Relationships together.

Table of Contents

The Foundations of Marriage 1

Foundation of Love: Gil & Renée Beavers... 2

Foundation of Fear: Gil & Renée Beavers... 9

The Framework of Marriage...................... 17

Marriage as An Act of Worship: Babbie Mason
.... 18

Beliefs: The Washington's 29

Personal Inventory: The Jefferson's.......... 36

Communication: The Cox's 44

Let's Talk: The Martin's 54

Expectations: The Randolph's................... 62

Love and Respect : The Garcia's............... 72

Personality Styles and Habits: The Evan's 81

Conflict Resolution: The Lachhu's............. 89

Generational Love: The Johnson's 98

Roles and Responsibilities: The Witherspoon's
.... 104

Blended Familia: The Rojas' 114

Love That Works: The Hoskins' 122

Marriage After Divorce: The Brown's 132

Marriage & Diversity: The Higby's 139

Friends and Family: The Riley's 149

Remote Love: The Pope's 159

Marriage & Ministry: The Allen's 170

Money Styles: Dr. White 179

Intimacy & Sex: Gil & Renée Beavers 187

Trust in Marriage: Gil & Renée Beavers . 198

Identity in Marriage: Gil & Renée Beavers203

Empathy in Marriage: Gil & Renée Beavers210

The Code Breaker in Marriage: PRIDE 217

The Code Breaker in Marriage – Pride: Gil & Renée Beavers 218

Marriage Prayers: Gil & Renée Beavers . 221

Prayer of Salvation: Gil & Renée Beavers226

The Foundations of Marriage

After working with many couples, we began to see a pattern. Everyone's marriage is built on something, Love or Fear. The choice is yours. Love is a solid foundation.

Foundation of Love:
Gil & Renée Beavers

"I need Love, Love..." Yes, we all need and want Love! Many of us have songs we love, and some could be our life anthems. Music reminds us of good and bad times; songs connect us to God and our humanity. There's a song by Tina Turner titled "What's Love Got to do With It?" This very question plagued me until I experienced Love for the first time. I learned that Love is the key to everything real and meaningful. Love, in many cases, has been mistaken by its imposter, lust.

Love, unlike lust, in my experience, gives. Love waits, Love opens doors. Love slips lunch money in your handbag at the age of nineteen when you are not looking. Love creates friendship and trust. Love requires time and patience. No, Love cannot pay the bills, yet Love is what we must live for at any cost. Love is a choice, not an emotion. The two of us have lived in the same home, and in different countries, we are proof that Absence only allows the heart to do what it is intended to do all along. What principles are we building our marriage on? When building a home, you begin with the foundation. Let's dig deep to look into the work our foundation requires.

Living on Love is the only way to truly thrive in our marriage. After doing hair and owning salons for twenty-eight years, you get to meet hundreds of women who openly share their stories with you.

After working with many couples, we began to see a pattern. Everyone's marriage is built on something, Love or Fear. The Choice is ours. Love is a solid foundation. My favorite and most life-changing bible verse is Romans 5:8 New International Version (NIV), "But God demonstrates His own love for us in this: While we were still sinners, Christ died for us." This verse is life giving, and it communicates unconditional Love and acceptance. When marriage is built on Love, serving one another is our only competition.

Love is a choice, not an emotion. God is Love, and since He is not one dimensional, neither is Love. Love has many facets. Here are seven different commitment levels within Love:

Agape — Unconditional Love

Eros — Romanic Love

Philia — Affectionate Love

Philautia — Self-love

Storge — Familiar Love

Pragma — Enduring Love

Ludus — Playful Love

While this list begins with the ending goal, which is agape, unconditional love, Love grows and has stages. Love for God and ourselves is paramount. John 15:12 says, "My command is this: Love each other as I have loved you."

I remember having someone explain to me that you can never love anyone until you love yourself. I am convinced the way we love ourselves will be the same way we love others. I believe God's love teaches us and increases our capacity to know, accept, and love ourselves and others. We must take the long journey inward to grow and change. Looking for growth areas in others is natural and comfortable.

When will we ask ourselves the hard questions like, "Who am I? Who told me that? Who hurt you?" Relationships are where we have the highest likelihood to grow if we are willing to do the work and Love. We have to unpack and examine ourselves. Working *in* your marriage begins with looking at the reflection in the mirror, while working *on* our relationship requires developing the necessary tools to make a healthy relationship our reality. Yes, healthy relationships require work, and that work begins with us.

Love matures and intensifies, much like a fire. How will you know if your marriage is built on Love? One of the most significant indicators of Love is the way we treat one another. One of the many acronyms we learned early was being H.O.T. Honest, open, and transparent. The marriage that is built on Love is H.OT. In our marriage, we have many principles that we have learned to live by. We learned this from one of the first couples we mentored during premarital counseling in Texas. Honest, Open, and Transparent means that you see and know yourself, and that you are willing to be open and vulnerable about your strengths, weaknesses, and growth areas. It's a great principle; I believe it's what keeps the fire in our marriage. Today, try to be H.O.T.! Sidebar, what this does not mean is that you look at the other person to find out their weaknesses, and growth areas; that is called being a hot mess!

LIVING FOR LOVE

What does that look like? How does one live for love? Living for love requires people, and living for love is not easy. Who can accomplish this lifestyle? Others must always come first. The concept of "Me, Myself, and I" must die. With this lifestyle, time, grace, and selflessness shapes us. The awareness that how we live affects others impacts our decision-making. You learn that everything and everyone is connected, and that today was a grown-up of yesterday. Our investments will yield a return. It takes three to make one person for a reason. Love is the fuel that moves us forward. Life is where we learn that our deepest needs are not things. Our greatest gains are wrapped up in our most painful losses. Living for love is a lifestyle of giving your all to others. Not because you want everything in return, but because God's love overflows each day and we don't want it to go to waste because of our selfish decisions. God has an endless supply! We have to allow Him to use us to lead others to Him with His love for a lifetime, now that's living!

READ ROMANS 15:7-8 KING JAMES VERSION (KJV)

7 Wherefore receive ye one another, as Christ also received us to the glory of God.

8 Now I say that Jesus Christ was a minister of the circumcision for the truth of God, to confirm the promises made unto the fathers...

So, reach out and welcome one another to God's glory.

Foundation of Fear:
Gil & Renée Beavers

FEAR has an enormous effect on the development and building of the healthiest of marriages. It is an emotion that, if kept to yourself without your partner ever really knowing what you are going through, can have consequences that you may be unaware of its origin.

Psalms 27:1 NIV states, "The Lord is my light and my salvation; whom shall I fear? The Lord is the stronghold of my life; of whom shall I be afraid?" When I first heard that scripture, I instantly thought about myself and how Fear was affecting my life. I felt like I walked in a constant state of being fearful, not of an accident, not of a tragedy, but of the uncertainties of what the future may hold for me. I once heard Fear being described as an acronym for false evidence appearing real. I could instantly relate to that acronym. The essence of Fear is insecurities, layered with self-doubt. It is rooted in my desire to control my life. Control of knowing that I must rely on God for my daily necessities of life. Fear handicaps growth in your marriage. One thing that attracted me to my wife was her constant state of being Joyful. This was something I lacked in my own life because Fear had me bond by thinking of my past that now affected my future and the future of my spouse. That "lack" that I was experiencing had its origin when I was a young child of a broken marriage and an absentee father. When you don't have a father who is your first provider in the physical realm, it sets the stage for Fear and doubts in my heavenly Father to be there when I needed Him. Prior to this, I never truly understood how my trust should not be in a person, but in the one and true Living God to provide for every area of my life.

The first thing that dissolves is joy. The lack of joy comes from the constant attention that you give to not having the things that are required for life as the Bible speaks about in Matthew 6:25, "Therefore I tell you, do not worry about your life, what you will eat or drink; or about your body, what you will wear. Is not life more than food, and the body more than clothes?"

As an individual or a married couple, you must be willing to take the longest journey inward and be truly honest with yourself. I realized I was Closed, Obstinate, Lazy, and Dishonest (C.O.L.D); not from the temperature outside, but neglect of my emotional health. I had allowed myself to be controlled by my old human nature versus my new life and the Holy Spirit. It was many years until I realize I had allowed Fear to keep me "closed" off from my spouse. I closed off areas that I didn't want to address. This was the first trait of being COLD. When you close off your emotions and feelings to the one you love, it sets up barriers that sometimes never disappear until you allow the Holy Spirit to reveal those barriers.

Next, I had to admit that I was obstinate, the second trait of being COLD. In simple terms, I was stubborn with myself. It can be more comfortable to hold on to areas of your life that you are satisfied with rather than change. You may feel your spouse needs to accept you just as you are.

However, when you commit your life to another person, the essence of growth has to be you being open to change the things that don't benefit the overall relationship. God placed this person in your life to help shape and mold you into the person He called you to be. If you are obstinate, you're hurting yourself and hindering your marriage from maturing.

The third trait in COLD is LAZY, which is closely associated with being obstinate. The very things that attracted you to your spouse can become what you like least when it is your growth area. You cannot allow complacency to become your default behavior.

Finally, when I examined my disposition and accepted that I was DISHONEST, I had to admit the source of my Fear, which is the "D" in COLD. I wasn't intentionally dishonest with my spouse. I was dishonest with myself. Sometimes it was conscious, but mostly it was my unconscious behavior, I had to be willing to answer the hard questions and speak the truth in love to my spouse. Not about her, but about me living in a state of Fear. Psalm 34 reads, "I sought the LORD, and he answered me and delivered me from all my fears." The beginning of getting over Fear as the Bible describes it, is seeking God and a relationship with the one and true living God.

If you have never surrendered your life to Christ Jesus, this is the beginning of the journey to eradicating Fear in your life. You will find a Salvation prayer at the end of this chapter. You can stop right now and go there and pray, then return to this section. The practice of GOD delivering you from Fear in your life starts with trust. Proverbs 3:5-7 says, "Trust in the Lord with all your heart, soul in mind, lean not on your understanding, acknowledge Him First, and he will direct your path. Do not be wise in your own eyes, fear the Lord and shun evil." This is critical to building the foundation of love, not only with your relationship with God, but also with your relationship with your spouse. You will never be able to overcome Fear and being COLD, if you don't love God! Then, you can't love yourself and ultimately find love in your spouse.

FEAR!

It's like darkness in a long cave with no end in sight. It's like an intense aroma in a small room with no windows. It's like being surrounded by bullies with no one to help. Fear has a power that makes you feel helpless and defeated. It can make an obvious answer complicated. Fear stands at the door of opportunity and tells you that you are not invited. From birth, we are all aware of fear. However, there are only two legitimate fears from birth: the fear of falling and the fear of loud noises. These fears, unfortunately, grow as we grow. The battle with fear is a lifelong struggle, and it begins and ends in our minds. Parents learn early that their fears are not theirs alone.

Conscious and consequently, fear is transferable. What an awful use of our influence! Our thoughts become words, which become habits, and our habits alter our character, which forms our life and our lifestyles. We do not have control over the thoughts that come to our minds. However, we are in control of how much and how long we entertain them. You have three choices if you walk into a room in your home and don't like what is on the television. Watch it and increase your exposure, change the channel, or leave the room. Fear is much like reality T.V.; it only receives renewals by massive amounts of viewers. No viewers, then the show is canceled or redirected from prime time to a less viewed channel. Fear only has as much power as we give it. Pull the plug on fear with hope and love; they are more beneficial gifts to our lives and our children.

Psalm 86:11-12 reads, "Teach me thy way, O Lord; I will walk in thy truth: unite my heart to fear thy name. I will praise thee, O Lord my God, with all my heart: and I will glorify thy name forevermore" (King James Version).

The Framework of Marriage

The framework is the critical component of your relationship that provides shape, structure, and shelter. Before a home is decorated and personalized, it has to be covered; this is what the framework provides for our marriage.

MARRIAGE AS AN ACT OF WORSHIP: BABBIE MASON

As I write this chapter, my heart turns to deep reflection. Forty years ago this month, my husband, Charles, and I stood at the altar and said, "I do." A lot of life can take place in forty years; the wedding, the honeymoon, getting acclimated to new jobs and a new city, buying a home, having children, vacations, celebrations, graduations, grandchildren, health challenges, marrying and burying, the empty nest and aging gracefully. The past four decades have been packed with lots of love and unforgettable memories as we continue to grow to know one another.

There were times of uproarious laughter. I'll never forget the day, as I was washing dishes at the kitchen sink, I looked out of the window that faced our backyard only to see my husband, Charles, and our two sons testing the bounce-ability of the trampoline he had just purchased, by jumping off the roof of our one-story ranch house. I don't recommend that! Praise the good Lord; everyone came through the adventure unscathed! We shed plenty of tears as we stood at the graveside of loved ones. Lots of prayers went up when our children left the nest and went out on their own, moving to faraway states. Our colorful back-story of faith and family has been the super glue that has held us together. We've discovered that a good marriage isn't something you find. It's something you make, and you must keep on making it into the kind of love story that makes God look good. One thing is for sure, we wouldn't have made it forty years without the Lord at the center of our home and our marriage.

You see, Charles and I are total opposites in pretty much every way. I am from the north while he is from the south. I'm from the city. Charles is a country boy, born and bred. I love being indoors with my second cup of coffee, reading or writing something inspirational, while Charles loves being outdoors working on our farm. (At this very moment, I am here in my writing room at the computer crafting this chapter. I just waved to Charles as he rode past the picture window on the lawn mower)! I love chocolate. He loves vanilla. Give me a sweet pickle. Charles has to have a dill. I love watching Jeopardy. Charles loves watching football. I enjoy driving a nice car; Charles makes his rounds in his old pickup truck. I love shopping and sight-seeing while Charles is perfectly happy people-watching from a park bench. When it came to raising our children, Charles laid down the law while I extended grace.

Being married to someone who is the exact opposite presents its challenges as far as personalities are concerned. I've often said, "Opposites attract, but if we're not careful, opposites can attack!" Granted, being married to someone who sees life through a different lens can cause some frustrations that can lead to sessions of head-butting and contentious push- back. Early in our marriage, we hardly agreed on anything. We went through years of nipping. and snipping at one another until we just got tired and wore one another down. To find peace in our home, we've had to learn big lessons about what it means to yield to each other. Philippians 2:3 says, "Do nothing out of selfish ambition or vain conceit. Rather, in humility, value others above yourselves" (New International Version).

There are many comparisons that can be made between marriage and worship. At the foundation of both worship and marriage, is humility and service. It took many years for Charles and me to learn this powerful lesson, because it is so natural for people to want things their way. There comes a time when your motivation is not getting your own way or having your own say, but pleasing Christ in every area of your relationship. Embracing this truth, not only has a plethora of advantages, it reaps a bounty of blessings. Like salt and pepper, day and night, darkness and light, fire and water, and rock hard and cottony soft, you need both elements to strike the perfect balance.

John chapter 4 speaks of this beautiful balancing act and of how important this balance is in worship. Let's look at this passage a little more closely to see the value of appreciating the gifts, talents, and perspectives that both husband and wife can bring to a marriage, and how seeing marriage in this regard can actually be an act of worship. In a conversation Jesus had with the Samaritan woman in John 4:21-24, Jesus said to her, "Woman, believe Me, the hour is coming when you will neither on this mountain nor in Jerusalem, worship the Father. You worship what you do not know; we know what we worship, for salvation is of the Jews. But the hour is coming, and now is, when the true worshipers will worship the Father in Spirit and truth; for the Father is seeking such to worship Him. God is Spirit, and those who worship Him must worship in Spirit and truth."

As a singer, songwriter, and author of Christian music and books, Charles and I have had the joy of working together in ministry in all kinds of settings for most of our marriage. My husband works diligently behind the scenes, while I step into my calling from the stage to lead people in times of worship. I have found that some define worship in terms of the style of music and songs. Some might define worship as singing, lifting our hands, bowing our heads, or some other outward display. While these external displays matter, that's not all there is. Worship is so much more than a song or a physical demonstration. Worship is the act of bowing down one's life in reverence and paying homage to God for Who He is and for all He has done. To worship, 'in spirit' means to bow down one's whole heart. Psalm 103:1 declares, "Bless the Lord, O my soul, and all that is within me, bless His holy name" (English Standard Version).

Just as in a healthy marriage, there is no real relationship without a devout commitment. It's impossible to worship God with a divided heart. What is required, is a life that is completely sold out. Jesus speaks of worship from two opposite perspectives; Spirit and truth. To worship God 'in spirit', implies that worship is not manufactured by some external force, but worship comes from deep within the heart, motivated by love and sincerity. When we worship 'in spirit,' we choose to worship as a way of living, making the decision to embrace the spirit-led life. Unless we are completely surrendered to God, there can be no worship in Spirit. It means giving the Holy Spirit access to every area of our lives. John 4:24 states that God is a spirit. This means He cannot be confined to one place or space. In the same way, our lives must no longer be compartmentalized, only giving to God a little space or span of time during a church service on the weekends, as if to check an obligation off of a to-do-list. But the one who lives life by the Spirit will not only make room for God, but that person will build an entire world around Him, making every moment of every day an act of worship. This passion for God should impact and influence everything we do and the way we live. Worship is not only an act, but one's life becomes a love song, bringing glory and honor to God in words and deeds.

We must also worship God 'in truth.' It's impossible to worship a God we don't know. Therefore, the first step to worshiping God 'in truth' is to endeavor to know the truth. We can practice this by spending time getting to know Him through the pages of His Word, the Bible. Instead of following after the ways of the world, when we spend time in God's Word, renewing our minds on a daily basis, we will follow what He says. Read Romans 12:1. "Therefore, I urge you, brothers and sisters, in view of God's mercy, to offer your bodies as a living sacrifice, holy and pleasing to God—this is your true and proper worship" (New International Version).

As we present our bodies to Christ, daily walking out our faith, the practice of our worship should reflect biblical truth. In 2 Timothy 3:16-17 the Bible reads, "All Scripture is God-breathed and is useful for teaching, rebuking, correcting, and training in righteousness, so that the servant of God may be thoroughly equipped for every good work."

Can you see how important it is that everything we say and do align with the truth of Scripture? The conversations we have, the posts we make on social media, the books we read, how we share our faith with others—truth is the measuring stick by which we live our lives. In the work Charles and I do, the deepest desire of our hearts is that our work brings glory to God. We hope to influence those we come in contact with to love Jesus deeper and know Him more intimately.

We are far from perfect, and we know there will always be room to grow in our faith. From the time I was a young believer, living for Christ and playing the piano in my Father's church, God's Word has had first place in my life. For Charles, who came to know Christ as a young adult, demonstrating what it looks like to be a godly husband and Father, is of utmost importance to him. Here's the point. If we want others to follow us into a deeper faith experience, then we have a responsibility to know and handle truth correctly. For some, a highly spirited, emotional relationship with God is important. A gamut of emotions often define the worship experience. For others, a focus on truth takes the lead. Acquiring knowledge and understanding theology defines that worship experience. According to John 4:21-24, it's not one over the other, but both are critical to growth and maturity for the believer.

I've often said like this: "Operate in the Spirit without the truth, and you blow up. Expound on the truth without the Spirit, and you dry up. But when the Spirit and the truth walk hand in hand, you grow up."

Here's the bottom line. I'm a witness that God can take a mess of a marriage and transform it into a living testimony. Whether you are married for a day or for decades, Jesus is all we need to be truly satisfied in life and love. It's not about who is right or who is wrong. It's not about getting our way or having our say. It's about being submitted and committed to Christ and to one another so that the Lord's name can be glorified. It's never too late to find that beautiful balance in marriage. It's worth fighting for. Both the husband and wife can contribute their unique gifts to create a marriage that pleases the Lord.

BELIEFS: THE WASHINGTON'S

We are Cedrick, and Emem Washington. Welcome to our life and our marriage message. Get ready! Emem: "I could not believe what he had just said to me. Had I heard right? Did he just mention the 'D' word to me?" A flood of thoughts and emotions swept over me, and I lashed out with some harsh words of my own. I told him to bring the papers, and I would gladly sign them. How did we end up in this place anyway, just four short months into our marriage?

CEDRICK:

As soon as I said it, I regretted it. But I was so angry and hurt, and I wanted her to hurt too. This was probably not going to last, I thought to myself. It seemed like she knew how to push my buttons, and so, even after having gone through pre-marital counseling sessions, I was no longer confident we'd make it to six months, let alone to "happily ever after."

BOTH:

Our family is blended, and we are blessed with five sons between us. We are so different from each other, and, for a while, we did not know how to handle that. Have you noticed that when you're courting, the differences you notice in each other seem so refreshing, and maybe even cute. But isn't it funny how, soon after you say, "I do," those very differences begin to put a wedge between you? What once was funny becomes annoying; what once impressed you about your spouse, now makes you wonder if you made the right decision.

We have experienced some steep valleys in our relationship. We have said and done extremely hurtful things to each other, in spite of the fact that we are believers and we know better. Not to mention the fact that we have both served in the church for a long time. Both of us come from previous relationships that did not work. We brought a lot of that baggage into our marriage, along with the typical growing pains that come with any relationship.

While we cannot (with straight faces) tell you that our marriage has been perfect, we can tell you that we have been able to find joy in our marriage and finally have peace in our home. We can confidently assure you that, no matter how challenging your situation might be, there is hope, and we are not saying that lightly. Today, our marriage is a source of care, comfort, mutual protection, and peace. We now have a deep love and respect for each other, and we are intentional about the words we use to and "about" each other.

How did we make the shift from almost filing for divorce (several times) to where we are today? We went back to our core spiritual beliefs. As different as we are, we share the same spiritual beliefs, and those beliefs have strengthened our bond and brought us closer together. We have learned to come back to those beliefs during difficult times.

Here are three of the spiritual beliefs that help guide us in our marriage:

Jesus is the head of our home. When you recognize and accept this, you place Jesus above yourself, your children, your job, and even your ministry. Jesus means more to you than your need to be right or to win the fight. This was something we both had to learn and remind ourselves of often. We both agree that we love God with all our heart, mind, soul, and spirit. The love we have for Him surpasses the love we have for each other, and it influences how we now speak to and respond to each other.

Putting God first also means that, rather than looking to your spouse to meet your emotional needs, you look to Jesus. Looking to another human being, no matter how loving he or she is, sets yourself up to be disappointed. Whether it is an affirmation that you need or encouragement, your spouse will not be able to give that to you always, and not in the way that God gives it.

Always remember who the real enemy is. You do have an enemy, but that enemy is not your spouse. Your common enemy is Satan. As God's word tells us, the enemy wants to steal, kill, and destroy, and he wants to do all of that in your marriage. Remembering this helps diffuse arguments and tense situations. We each come from different backgrounds and have experienced different things. So, we will not always see eye to eye, but that does not make us enemies.

Choose to die daily. This is discussed by the apostle Paul in 1 Corinthians 15:31. Dying daily is not an easy thing to do. In fact, when our pastors/spiritual mentors first started teaching us about this concept of dying daily (during the many sessions they have had with us after we got married), neither one of us knew exactly how to live it out. To be honest, we were hung up on the word "die." What did it mean to die daily?

Dying daily means that we die to ourselves, our rights, and our desire to be right. When we are dead to everything around us, we have no personal rights or agendas. When you die to self, you don't focus on what he is doing wrong or what she is not doing right. It helps you to focus on the positive aspects of each other and to encourage and respect each other. When you die daily, it becomes easier to be the bigger person and ask forgiveness of your spouse, even when you believe that your spouse is in the wrong. You relate with your spouse from a place of compassion, not pride or ego. In dying to self, we truly live.

We are grateful that our Father in heaven is a God of second chances. He has been our Redeemer in many ways. Just as He did not give up on us, we will not give up on each other. When we took a closer look at our common spiritual beliefs, we made the firm decision to keep God first, to focus on the real enemy, and to die to self, which has enabled us to overcome the challenges. No marriage is perfect, but by the grace of God, we are in a great place, for which we give God all the glory!

What are some of your spiritual beliefs? Take the time to dig deep and discover the beliefs you both share that can serve as your compass during difficult times. We are rooting for you!

Personal Inventory:
The Jefferson's

Have you ever been to a wedding and observed the unity candle being lit by both parties? That is our favorite part of witnessing a wedding. We love the significance and symbolism the unity candle represents in a marriage. Two flames are fizzling out just as they spark a more significant fire. The two flames were the lives they once knew. Now, the united flame represents the support and love for one another through the good times and the bad. Although, when those two candles are united, with them, they bring experiences, hurts, needs, and other baggage that must be affectionately sorted out. This personal inventory is what makes each marriage unique. Welcome to marriage!

As a couple, we deal with certain situations in a myriad of ways. Our past involvements create memories. These memories are pleasant and unpleasant. We try to hold on to the good ones, but the bad ones leave scars and build layers around our minds and hearts. When we remove those layers, only then could the core of who we are, begin to emerge. In other words, personal inventory enabled us to reveal who we indeed are and foreshadowed how we react to various circumstances.

Along with communication, personal inventory is vitally important to a marriage, because it can be used to peel away those layers. Your spouse does not know what your needs are nor how to handle them if you do not tell them. Therefore, taking a personal inventory of yourself is crucial. You must identify your basic needs and the nuances of who you are in order to communicate with your mate effectively. We have to ask ourselves, "What are my aspirations that bring me hope? What motivates me? What satisfies the innermost desires within me? and How do these aspects fall in line with my Christian values and those of my spouse? How can we merge them and live on one accord?"

As a couple, we have always relied on Christ as a constant. He is a compass that has provided us with direction, that led us through times of anger, mistrust, and malalignment in our belief system. "Let love and faithfulness never leave you; bind them around your neck, write them on the tablet of your heart. Then you will win favor and a good name in the sight of God and man. Trust in the Lord with all of your heart and lean not on your own understanding; in all your ways submit to him, and He will make your paths straight" (Proverbs 3:3-6).

Once the personal inventory has taken place, the submission of personal values, traits, and habits come into play. Coming from different homes, religious backgrounds, and other avenues of life's journeys, couples coming together as one unit can often undergo an uphill battle that can annihilate many marriages. Having disagreements in areas such as where you plan to go to church, how to discipline your children, how to spend or save money are all factors that can lead your marriage to its demise. For us, an instance of submission occurred one Sunday morning, as we were driving to attend a church service. We were running late for an intended location, and I was not in total agreement with the denomination of this church nor its teachings. We were in a dark place in our relationship, and after ten years of marriage at the time, we were at wit's end on the subject. Then, out of nowhere, the Lord placed it in my heart to concede. If I were to be obedient to my Father in Heaven, then I must submit to His will and His way. When this happened, I spoke out and told my husband I give it over to him. I will no longer resist or cause contention in the marriage in this aspect. He then turned into the parking lot of another church that he had been invited to months prior to this incident. Through faith, we placed membership after our 3rd visit and have grown there for over ten years. My submission led to more significant relations between us as a couple and our children's baptisms. Ephesians 5:21 states, "Submit to one another out of reverence for Christ" (New International Version).

Therefore, both parties must submit. If the husband expects his wife to submit to him, he must show her how to surrender by yielding to Christ. After all, Christ set the example of how to care for your wife by the way He cared for the church and gave himself up for her.

As we have taken inventory of ourselves throughout the years, we learned that communication is the key that unlocks the door to success in every relationship, whether it is a personal or a business relationship. With us both having management experience and entrepreneurial spirits, we have found that communication reveals undiscovered paths that couples will venture through. They would have to identify what satisfies each of their essential needs and enables them to achieve like-mindedness. For us, communication comes not only in the form of speaking but also in our body language, our time present with each other, and our ability to simply listen. A spouse should listen not needing to be right or proving the other wrong, but genuinely hearing to understand what the other party is trying to say. For example, my wife told me about the issues she was having at work. I was so intent on resolving the issue for her, that I did not realize that she just needed me to listen to her vent. She would solve the problem independently, but she needed me to make her feel like someone was on her side. Throughout her developing years, she was frequently told to be quiet or shut up. She was made to feel like her opinion did not matter. After this was communicated to me, I better understood why she felt the way she did, what she was going through, and how to handle the situation. By paying attention to the various ways we communicate, we have conquered many big and small conflicts. Communication can be used in conflict resolution.

As a couple, we have learned each other's love language and are cognizant of times when the other is upset or frustrated. It is our agreement that we are not allowed to stay angry for a prolonged period. We converse with each other to resolve the issue with a solution that fits our shared habit of not going to bed mad. The scripture, Ephesians 4:26 (NIV) says, "Do not let the sun go down on your wrath." This scripture has been at the forefront of all our interactions with each other. In effect, when we take a personal inventory of who we are and consult the Lord through prayer and petition, we bring our vulnerabilities, our triumphs, and our defeats with open and honest communication to our relationship.

This impacted our marriage significantly, by allowing us to be conscientious of our spouse's core needs and handle each other's well-being with a Christ-like mindset. Therefore, couples must tear down their individual preconceived notions of what a marriage should look like. Self-reflect on what makes you who you are. Then, together as a couple, take it to Jesus, from which all knowledge and wisdom flow. "Finally, brothers, whatever is true, whatever is noble, whatever is right, whatever is pure, whatever is lovely, whatever is admirable—if anything is excellent or praiseworthy—think about such things. Whatever you have learned or received or heard from me or seen in me — put it into practice. And the God of peace will be with you" Philippians 4:8-9 (NIV).

Communication:

The Cox's

"Death and life are in the power of the tongue: and they that love it shall eat the fruit thereof" (Proverbs 18:21 NKJV).

Out of the abundance of the heart, the mouth speaks is a familiar Bible verse. What if the heart refuses to speak, can't speak, or the heart hasn't any faith in the exchange between their spouse? They love each other, but they can't manage consistent, productive conversations. A lack of healthy communication was our reality for a long time during our marriage. We had a heck of a time conflating, combining individual narratives to a connected whole. We are humbled to share with you the major factors that contributed to our dysfunctional discourse.

Early in our marriage, we realized that we were not on the same page when communicating how we felt or what we needed from one another. Most of the problem was our immaturity. We were not fortunate to witness blissful relationships/marriages growing up. We exercised a few unsuccessful problem-solving communicative techniques such as arguing loudly with venom, but found that it wasn't our style, so we tried a more refined approach, restraining our volume, but with venom. Keep reading because we have more to share about what you don't want to nurture as a common practice in your marriage when it comes to communicating with your life partner.

A brief description of us is essential to understand how our communication issues escalated us to silence. Bartees is an only child that left home for a career in the Air Force at the age of eighteen. While in the military, he lost thirty percent of his hearing due to his occupation as an aircraft mechanic. His approach to communication is mostly straightforward and simple, not a lot of words, a kind of get to the point person. Donna is the youngest of three sisters, a singer, and an educator. She believes in talking it out until a solution surfaces and feels that sharing her interpretation of an issue is paramount. Yes, she is an "express yourself kind of woman" with high emotions. We clashed because we did not consistently execute justly the delivery of our feelings (an individuals' interpretation of what 'I am' experiencing). Mannerisms made us respond adversely to one another, like smiling during serious conversations, answering the phone, and the one we latched on to keep the peace in our home, silence.

Because Bartees did not have siblings to hash out problems, he profoundly practiced shutting down rather than talking. Partially because of his upbringing and because I talked a lot. When Bartees shut down, I learned to give him space. Giving him space turned into days and eventually, a host of unresolved issues between us. We did not want to argue, which meant we did not solve any of our issues. Bartees felt that since our words were unproductive, "Why keep talking, because nothing is going to change?" I stopped pursuing him to talk because I did not know how to verbally interact with him without feeling worse after another unresolved issue. Eventually, we would go on as if the area of contention disappeared. Little by little, the silence we nurtured interfered with intimacy in our relationship.

Another common practice that surfaced regularly in our marriage was referring to the past. Relating repetitive problems and how it correlated to what we were going through was Donna's way of resolving some core issues. Sometimes those were my intentions. There were other times that I referred to the past with another reason. Remember that venom I mentioned earlier. Well, I also brought up the past when I wanted to throw some venom if I'd been hurt during a disagreement. I never thought about how it crippled our relationship. Those episodes left Bartees emotionally drained, and we were not getting anywhere. So, if I referenced the past, it made him feel like he was fighting a losing battle. Bringing up the past for us, stole the sovereignty of forgiveness between us.

My choices and behavior's name are unforgiveness. Unforgiveness was my personal experience with my feelings that I employed to punish Bartees self-indulgently. Whether that was my intention or not, it was the product of it. It comes to a point in a relationship that having secret grudges and resentments have to be replaced by forgiveness God's way. Forgiveness consists of two elements: words and actions. If words 'I forgive you' are not followed through with the steps that follow, the words are most important. Referring to the past must be done appropriately, but if the motive is not right, it does more damage to the relationship.

Other reasons got in the way of our facing one another to talk, but the two areas we mentioned in this setting wreaked the most havoc in our lives. We learned from our past and exercised a new liberty every day to live lovingly healthy. Recognizing why prayer is essential in our individual life helped us get to a place of longing for reconciliation. Let's back up a bit more to show how confessing Christ as our Lord and Savior changes a person's life. We hear about salvation and confess with faith that we accept salvation. Then we are encouraged to share what happened to provoke us to accept salvation. Someone prays with us, and we are saved. We are encouraged to pray because it's part of building our relationship with God as well as keeping us connected to our Source. We do not think it is a coincidence that prayer, conversing with God, is highly encouraged by God, pastor, and teachers of the Bible. Geez, look at how many books were written and prayer groups across the globe practice prayer for their close relationships with God? Why would we think that a marriage doesn't need consistent discourse to sustain our relationship and intimacy? We converse with God daily, so you have to converse with your spouse daily to sustain a lively, healthy, vulnerable relationship! We have some simple daily practices that assist us in maintaining peaceful discourse. Below are some areas to remember so that you are changing the atmosphere in your home:

Words have power. The power of the choice of words and how we say words (i.e., accusatory vs. inquiring); catty (to be hurtful) vs. a discussion; argumentative vs. communicating. Men: Do not say the first thing that comes to mind if it is going to sound misogynistic.

Women: Learn how to think past your emotions. So, think before you speak. Be mindful of the words and the tone, because it might not be received the way you thought it was delivered.

Communication is a two-way exchange: Premising a conversation with "I have something to say, but I don't want to talk about it" can turn out one or two ways. First, we have to ask the question: Is this a fair exchange? What are you thinking about? Do not withhold what you think when a conversation could clear up unanswered questions? Communicating with personal barriers only turns into unresolved fights.

Listening with your emotions: Don't let your emotions dictate how and what you say. An emotional conversation is often unbiased. Meaningful discourse occurs when two people voice their opinions or the way something that made them feel a certain way.

Vulnerability: Not communicating is a sign of a couple's reluctance to be vulnerable. Vulnerability is not a sign of weakness but rather a sign of the strength of being respected and honored.

Practice listening empathetically: Usually, in an intense conversation, each person wants to be heard, and no one is listening. Someone must stop and listen, repeat what was said to ensure understanding and work together for a resolution.

Your relationship is worth fighting for, unless there are extenuating circumstances that prohibit your safety in any way. Talking can be a blessing or a curse to any relationship. We admonish you to talk through your problems or suffer the consequences. If you are having a tough time facing your spouse, allowing yourself to yield to vulnerability, and verbally expressing yourself, GET SOME HELP! An individual with experience and the intelligence to assist you through a drought season regarding communication, does not mean that you are incapable of correcting this error, but a little help can enhance your efforts.

Our journey of thirty-six years is a testament that we can do all things through Christ that strengthens us. As a couple, we are still finding our way together. We decided to commit ourselves further to learn how and nurture empathetic listening. Allowing ourselves to accept the blessing of vulnerability, reconnected a detectable level of compatibility and intimacy so much that we are experiencing what two now mature married lovers deserve. The covenant we took when we married one another was the only thing holding us together at times. Learning to communicate affects our daily disposition. We are committed to letting the fruit of the Spirit have free rein so that joy, kindness, peace, patience, self-discipline, and the greatest one of all, love, reconcile and resurrect our marriage. We want a better life for our children and their children's relationships. We still have work to do on this side of heaven for ourselves and our family.

"Communication is a key tool in a family's shared bond." Bartees & Donna Cox

LET'S TALK: THE MARTIN'S

We are Marcus and Zion. We've been married for three years, but in a relationship for almost eight. We have learned that words are powerful and how important talking and listening can be in a relationship. We hope that sharing some of our challenges and what we did to overcome them, blesses you and gives you another tool to help you build a stronger, healthier relationship.

People often say we need to talk through our issues, but it's hard to communicate when barriers are in place. Talking can be a wonderful tool to build up or tear down relationships. Did you know the same elements in Nitroglycerin, used to help alleviate chest pains in angina patients, can be used to create dynamite? When we talk, it can work for or against us, much like Nitroglycerin. Effective communication is needed to foster relationships, build bonds, and create intimacy. If you truly want to have intimate communication, you will have to be willing to let down your defenses and expose some of your vulnerabilities.

When Zion and I met, we started as friends sharing so many things about our past experiences and future goals. The more we talked, the more we found ourselves becoming trusting of each other. Before we knew it, we were dating and sharing more personal details about ourselves. The more we talked, the closer we became. Throughout the course of our relationship, we began to feel like communication was one of our strengths. As humans, when we reach a certain point, we believe we have conquered certain obstacles, creating an illusion of "that's behind me now." The enemy wants you to believe effective communication is no longer an obstacle in your relationship.

Over the course of our relationship, I felt like I could tell Marcus anything because he attentively listened to me. He gave me that warm and fuzzy feeling anytime I wanted to talk to him, and he also gave me appropriate feedback. Once, Marcus and I were talking on our cell phones, and there was an interruption that cut off part of what he was saying. That small part that was now missing, completely changed the message he was trying to relay. My response was still applicable, but not in the manner he expected. He was confused by my response, which spun us into a very uncomfortable conversation.

Zion led me to believe that I could be open and joke with her about anything. We would often text and talk throughout the day. That was until I sent her a text message that was misinterpreted. Further messages to clarify, only seemed to make the situation worse. I had upset her and didn't understand how, so I retreated and decided to stop talking, not to make matters worse. These are examples of incidents that hurt our communication and caused us to retreat within ourselves. Now we were not talking as openly, and instead, kept some feelings and concerns to ourselves.

The foundation that we felt was our strength, started to feel unstable. Suddenly other relationships seemed to look so much better than ours, especially when everyone was all smiles on social media. They didn't appear to have any problems, not anything big enough to relate to our "real" problems. This type of thinking is only a trick of the enemy to keep you isolated.

Zion and I found ourselves sinking in solitude. We weren't talking anymore, and when we did, it was as cordial and cold as two strangers.

Marcus felt very heavy in his demeanor and I think he sensed my sadness. One night, he asked me to take a ride with him. When I got in the car, he asked if I could put my phone in the armrest so we would have no distractions and just talk. It was hard, but I prayed and trusted God to cover me in my fears and be with Marcus as I spoke to him and as he spoke to me. We talked and we listened. This was one of the most impactful conversations we've had. It was like God turned the light on and Marcus was able to understand and see things clearer. By the time we got home we were a different couple than when we left. His demeanor was much lighter, and my sadness was gone. Instead of just being cordial, we were laughing and truly talking about things. God made a 180-degree pivot in our marriage that came about because we trusted Him as we listened to one another and talked.

It's easy for Marcus and me to carry on casual conversations like getting the car dropped off for maintenance and what we are having for dinner. However, it can be difficult to speak honestly, openly and/or transparently about uncomfortable issues dealing with our marriage. Neither of us wants to feel like we are nitpicking, so we sometimes keep things to ourselves. Allowing things to fester can make it worse. Withdrawing into solitude is a trick of the enemy. Hebrews 10:25 tells us not to forget about meeting together and Ecclesiastes 4:9 tells us that we are better together. When we share our struggles, it encourages others to share their testimony, which gives us strength and hope. This creates a community of couples helping couples, building strong, healthy, and loving relationships. Together we can help mend broken marriages.

Zion and I worked through some of our challenges by surrounding ourselves with like-minded couples who were willing to share their testimonies. We attended a Marriage small group from our church. We were a bit uncomfortable because we didn't know anyone, but we knew we didn't need to remain in isolation. Revelation 12:11 says we overcome the enemy by the power of our testimony. Hearing other couples' stories helped us realize what we were experiencing in our marriage was not uncommon. This gave us hope and encouragement that we could overcome what we were going through. We talked about various topics like ex-spouses and long-distance relationships.

Surround yourself with loving couples that seem to have the relationship that you wish to build with your spouse. We need each other for wisdom, guidance, and support. Don't be afraid to be honest, open, and transparent in your discussions about the things concerning you. Proverbs 27:17 tells us that iron sharpens iron, meaning we need the godly counsel of each other. You may need to seek godly counsel from a spiritual advisor to gain perspective and gather your own thoughts, and that's okay. We sometimes need others to tell us when we are wrong, when we are right, and how to speak encouragement and strength into our spouse's spirit. We have to understand that our spouses' differences are probably what made us fall in love with them. If we can learn to nurture those differences and speak in a manner that our spouses interpret as love, support, and understanding, we can heal and be healed.

Practice praying before speaking with your spouse; then, ask God to speak through you so your spouse will be receptive. Just remember talking is volatile. Talking can blow up and scar both of you, if not partnered with listening to understand. However, when properly handled and nurtured, communication becomes the fuel that burns inside the closest most intimate relationships. When you are ready, let's talk.

EXPECTATIONS: THE RANDOLPH'S

"Better is the end of a thing than the beginning thereof: and the patient in spirit is better than the proud in spirit" (Ecclesiastes 7:8).

OUR BEGINNING

We are Thaddeus and Amanda Randolph. We've been married for thirty-four years and have two wonderful sons. In the beginning, neither one of us truly understood what being married meant, nor do we now have it all figured out. But faith, family, and covenant are essential to us. Both of us grew up in single-parent homes without a Christian model of marriage. The first Christian marriage modeled before us came from our spiritual parents in the faith. As young Christians, we desired to make our marriage last because we wanted to break the cycle of poor choices in our families. We are taking the lessons we've learned and sharing them with other couples through a Marriage Mentor program we started in our local church. Walking in marriage for thirty-four years has had its challenges, but understanding and managing our expectations has helped us tremendously.

Some couples have expectations of large extravagant wedding ceremonies where they spend months and thousands of dollars planning for the big day. The vision of their perfect union may originate from a favorite fairy tale, movie, or magazine article. That is not our story, and it may not be yours. When we married, we had no big dreams or expectations for a large wedding ceremony. We just wanted to get married and have it last. We both had relatives who were married; however, none of them modeled a Christian marriage.

We met and married while serving overseas in the Republic of South Korea. You may think, "Wow, that's awesome." It is, and we love sharing our story because it's a great discussion starter with couples in our Relationship Coaching and Mentoring sessions. When we married, we had to request and get authorization from our chain of command. As dutiful soldiers, we requested and received permission.

When we received the approved paperwork, we went to the local Korean Municipal City Hall to get our paperwork stamped. At that point, we were only legally married in Korea. Next, we went to the United States Embassy in Seoul, Korea, to get the US stamp of approval and to file our paperwork with the State Department. No fanfare, no ticker tape, no rice or confetti. We walked out of the

Embassy, looked at each other, and said, "That's it. We're married now." We didn't stand before clergy or a justice of the peace and say, "I DO." All we knew, was that we were husband and wife. We thought we would move in together and go on as though we were dating. Little did we know that our expectations of what our marriage would be varied so differently.

FOUNDATIONAL EXPECTATIONS

What are expectations and how are they formed? The online dictionary defines expectations as a strong belief that something will happen or be the case in the future. For many, if not all, our expectations for marriage were formed by our childhood or youthful experiences. Our introduction to marital expectations is through our parents or guardians. As we grew older, beliefs and values mold our expectations. Societal norms and television also shape our expectations.

For example, young girls are socialized to look for "prince charming" and the "happily ever after" through movies such as Cinderella, Sleeping Beauty, Beauty and the Beast, or The Princess and the Frog. Each of these movies condition women to expect certain things from courtship and marriage. On the other hand, young men are socialized to relationships and manhood through games such as cops and robbers, cowboys and Indians, and various sports. The former perspective develops the ideas of comparison and completion, while the other produces the concepts of comparison and competition. How do we get these divergent perspectives to merge? We first have to realize that comparison can be an enemy to greatness, and competition can be an enemy to unity. At the same time, completion is a misnomer outside of Christ. You may ask, "What does this have to do with expectations?" When we enter into marriage, we are entering into a covenant relationship with one another. This covenant is a contractual agreement with built-in hopes of fidelity, intimacy, security, financial support, mutual trust, and care. When built-in expectations are unmet, a breeding ground for disappointment and marital dissatisfaction develops.

THE GREAT DIVIDE

"The greater the distance between expectations and reality, the greater the conflict." - Sam Chand

Through the years, we've learned that unspoken expectations in a marriage relationship can lead to conflict. We have coached many couples who come to us with communication and conflict resolution challenges and find out that most of the problem centers on their expectations. Each spouse enters into the marriage relationship with their expectations of sex, finances, roles, and responsibilities. There are also expectations on the number of children and extended family involvement in the relationship.

We each view and prioritize these expectations differently. When we don't communicate them to our spouse or significant other, these unspoken expectations may go unmet. So often, one or both spouses expect the other to know what they want either by osmosis or telepathy.

But, neither have that capability. When expectations are unspoken, unclear, or unrealistic, they can lead to frustration and low marital satisfaction. We often quote Sam Chand in telling couples the distance between expectation and reality is conflict.

MANAGE YOUR EXPECTATIONS

"So shall the knowledge of wisdom be unto thy soul: when thou hast found it, then there shall be a reward, and thy expectation shall not be cut off (Proverbs 24:14).

Communicate: Communication brings clarity. For example, when I first started playing golf, Amanda had expectations of me returning home at a specific time. Her expectation was for me to be gone for about three hours, and no more. As time went on, she learned eighteen holes of golf take about 4.5 hours, and nine holes take 2.5 hours.

There would be times, I would stop to get something to eat, or spend some time with the guys and not return home at her expected time. That caused conflict, especially if she cooked dinner or made plans for us to do something together. Both of us had to learn to communicate what our expectations were pertaining to golf. This lesson taught us how critical communicating expectations are in a relationship.

Allow space for grace and flexibility: Unmet expectations can lead to hurt and disappointment. When that happens, the offended spouse can either choose to hold or grant forgiveness. We've had multiple opportunities to be disappointed with each other. When we let disappointment set in, our hearts hardened against each other, and granting forgiveness was difficult. In each instance, the Holy Spirit reminds us of Ephesians 4:31-32, which tells us to put aside revenge, bitterness, and anger and instead to forgive just as Christ has forgiven us. Through more than thirty years of marriage, our expectations of each other have changed with the season in which we find ourselves.

Compliments and Positive Reinforcements: "Honey, I appreciate you doing that for me," goes much further than "Why didn't you take out the trash this morning?" Acknowledging your spouse's efforts is like a soft answer turns away wrath (Proverbs 15:1). When we repeatedly harp on what our spouse is not doing, it sends a message that we do not appreciate the effort they are putting forth. A little appreciation goes a long way in breaching a divide caused by negative comments. Proverbs 25:11 says, "A word fitly spoken is like apples of gold in pictures of silver." We encourage you to read this scripture in the Message Bible, which evokes the symbolism of the day we said, "I Do" and reinforces the love and appreciation we have for one another.

Finally, every couple enters into marriage with expectations. Those expectations are kind of like that old 70's ketchup commercial with the line from the Carly Simon song which says,

"Anticipation is making me late. Is keeping me waiting." Visualize if you will, you want ketchup for your hot, juicy hamburger or hotdog, and you have to wait for the ketchup. When the ketchup finally emerges and hits the hamburger or hotdog, you know the taste is worth the wait. Well, marriage is a lot like that. Many are familiar with Proverbs 13:12 (NIV) which states, "Hope deferred makes the heart sick, but a longing fulfilled is a tree of life." The Passion Translation evokes the imagery of someone falling into depression as they wait for their dreams to come true. But when they do, their soul is delighted and full of joy. We've learned, and so can you that managing expectations can lead to a healthy, happy, satisfying marriage relationship.

LOVE AND RESPECT: THE GARCIA'S

We are Edmund and Iris Garcia from Pearland, Texas, we have been married for fourteen years and have been serving as associate pastors at Greater Works Ministries for over twelve years. In the beginning, we believed that we could create a fairy tale of memories in a relationship that refused to allow God to lead. It is incredible how God has a sense of humor and will always get the last word, whether we like it or not. We have found that our unique backgrounds cultivated a peculiar formula that allowed God to get His Glory.

As you can imagine, throughout our years of marriage, Edmund and I have endured and overcome our portions of struggles. I came from a broken home at the early age of five-years old. As a child, my memories of my father and mother together were very vague. Coming from a family of very influential, strong, successful, and independent women, it was effortless to adapt to the mindset of not needing a man in place to lead. That would later create many challenges in our marriage. I grew up not truly understanding the importance of father figures. I was often left covering my brother, since my mother was the primary breadwinner for the family.

As I grew into a young adult, I found myself in and out of relationships, broken marriages that ended in divorce, leaving me broken from the loss. Despite it all, I continued to seek after the heart of God. Naturally, when it comes to advocating for children and fostering children, I learned quickly to make lemonade out of a lemon.

My mother instilled in me the gift of nurturing. I would always find ways to help assist single parents in fostering their children through difficult times. However, my father instilled in me the Word of God. My earliest memories of my father were filled with him teaching me how to memorize scripture and lean on God's Word. Unfortunately, in my young, teen, and adult years, I found myself running far away from God. The very thought of going to church, would literally make me sick to my stomach. It was not until after I turned thirty-years old that I realized there was a dark past that I was running from, but not before tying the knot with Edmund. It was not until the second year of marriage, I realized I needed to surrender and give my life back to Christ Jesus. During this time, while in prayer on a Saturday afternoon, the Holy Spirit began to reveal to me that I had been carrying a past filled with traumatic memories of being severely molested at the age of five by two women in the "church" daycare. That made for a long road to recovery. Still, that clearly exposed why my challenges for respect in my marriage consistently remained. I was hopeful that, nevertheless, God would be glorified through it all.

Edmund, story is different. I am from a Hispanic family. My parents migrated from Honduras in the mid to late 70's in pursuit of the American dream. The Hispanic culture is rich in tradition and family values. My parents have been married for nearly forty years, and neither parent had ever been divorced. The Hispanic culture is huge in letting the men lead the family and huge on loyalty and respect, which contributed significantly to my genetic makeup. My parents are also pastors at their local Hispanic church, which further instilled ethics and morals into me. Being product of a stable home made it easy to believe that I would've quickly acclimated to marriage life. However, as much as me parents worked to educate and nurture my physical, spiritual, and educational gifts, I never really witnessed my parents display much public affection for each other, which would later create a problem within my marriage. I know that my parents love each other. However, the absence of display or love hindered my understanding of love in my marriage. I never witness my parents make out, cuddle, or hold hands while walking in public places or even out to a movie. My father is a great man, but I never witnessed my father romance my mother in front of me. This lack of experience in my life would often lead to arguments and unmet needs down the road with Iris. I would come to understand that love is respect and respect is love, and for my marriage to survive, I would have to dig deeper with this phrase and learn to implement it in my daily life.

Many often believe that many years of marriage symbolizes a healthy union, but not in our case. We were too exhausted to throw in the towel. In the beginning stages of our marriage, we repeatedly fought often, ending in throwing things at each other. I damaged or punched a hole in the walls at our home. It was not uncommon to hear us yelling obscenities at each other. It was like hell on earth for the two of us. What had started as a beautiful friendship quickly soured into something unrecognizable, and more importantly, it did not glorify God. Both of us had to come to the humbling realization that we married each other for reasons other than love. Our foundation on which our marriage was founded had to be completely torn up. It was time to make a change.

We could have easily been embarrassed by such a revelation, but instead, we decided to admit our faults and enroll in counseling. We had to figure out why Iris lacked respect for Edmund and why I, was withholding love from Iris. Through years of counseling with our Overseer, Bishop Shon Gray at Greater Works Ministries, we identified the source of many issues plaguing our marriage. It was also during this time we learned to repent from our previous decisions for marriage. The bible says in 1 Cor. 11:28, "But let a man examine himself..." at that time, this seemed like a huge pill to swallow, but we understood it was necessary to begin the healing process. Admittance was one thing, but repentance was another.

I was able to identify that my upbringing without an active father in my life and coming from a line of dominant women contributed to a lack of respect towards men and Edmund did not witness much affectionate love between his parents, and it resulted as a form of withholding love in our marriage. The bible also teaches us in Ephesians 5:33, "Nevertheless, each individual among you also is to love his own wife even as himself, and the wife must see to it that she respects her husband." These were Godly principles that we did not bring into our marriage. Nevertheless, we both were willing, and in our willingness, we began to cultivate a lifestyle of surrender. We came to an even greater understanding that we both brought our own issues into our marriage, and truly were operating by our own strength and not God's Strength. However, God is so good.

We now know and understand that marriage is for the believer. Even though we entered the marriage having knowledge of God from being pastors' children, we indeed did not have a genuine relationship with the Creator. We found out quickly that lust is temporal, but love is everlasting. A wife being able to respect her husband is a mandate; it is not a choice or an option; it is The Word of God. Respect does not always mean you will have the last word, or get your way. It means that you understand the grace of submission. Submission is to lift up, support, and pray. Respect is being able to recognize that The Spirit of God rests and dwells within you both and subjecting your emotions and feelings to the Presence of God at all times.

A husband being able to love his wife is a mandate; it is not a choice or an option. It is The Word of God. Love is being patient, kind, gentle, slow to speak, and quick to listen. It is understanding how to meet the needs of your significant other without delay. We must understand that before we minister and love the world, we must know how to love our neighbor.

We say all of this to say, we have grown tremendously. Are we there yet? Absolutely not. Are we willing to allow God to continue to strengthen, blossom, and groom our relationship? Absolutely! We encourage others to always to do the same. God is love, and His love is to be respected. He desires to see us be made whole and ever fulfilled.

Dedication: We would like to dedicate our story to our Greater Works Ministries family and especially Bishop Shon Gray, who has stood beside us in our ugliest moments and reminded us who God called us to be together.

Acknowledgment: We would like to acknowledge our parents, family, friends and most of all our four beautiful daughters Kyra, Cameron, Elle, and Ava.

PERSONALITY STYLES AND HABITS: THE EVAN'S

When you have been married as long as we have, it is safe to say that basic personality styles and traits between spouses have pretty much been exposed. Many young couples get married today, and as soon as they have completed their vows, one insists on trying to "change" the other. We are Frank and Daphne Evans. We've been tested over and over, and for thirty-four years, we've managed to pass the test. We get promoted every year by adding another anniversary, and we consistently feel blessed that God has given us a path to love, understand and be patient with one another in our similarities and especially in our differences. Here is the first thing we've learned:

Rule number one in marriage- The weather changes, people don't.

When you stop and realize the essence of what attracts you to another person, the most important thing is to spend time and cultivate that attraction. Through careful, meaningful fun and interaction, you learn whether or not the personality is for you. Trying to be with someone because of their looks and not how they treat you, or equally as important, how you feel when you are with them is the main ingredient for a disastrous relationship. Being with someone strictly because of the monetary gain you may be able to realize from their company, is to the same degree, horrendous for future happiness. Finding that special thread that links commonalities or complements a difference, is the key to longevity and satisfaction between two people. We just managed to navigate that thread, weaving it in and out of good times and bad-when we completely understood the personality with which we were dealing as well as when we thought we were living with an alien from another planet. Sometimes we wonder exactly what has made us "click," and it is truly the basis in Romans 12:10, which says, "Be devoted to one another in love. Honor one another above yourselves," that allows us to function.

When you get right down to it, we really love one another. And, the funny thing is, we don't "wallow" in our love, we just know that it exists. But, our personalities are truly somewhat different. Frank is a thinker. He carefully mulls almost everything over in his mind-no matter what it is. Seldom making quick decisions, he is careful and weighs the pros, the cons, the opportunities, the strengths of every scenario in which he may come into contact. I, on the other hand, depend on my gut. I see something, I decide pretty quickly if it's a go or no. Now, that doesn't mean that I don't think about or consider important decisions over time, but my strength is my ability to see it and decide on viability.

Now, if you can imagine how the two of us have functioned with huge decisions like buying a house, I'm jumping up and down that this is a go, this is the house, let's make it happen while Frank is still stuck on whether or not it really is the right street, it makes for some challenging moments. That means I have to slow down and wait patiently for the stars, moon, and public transportation to all align before I can just tell the realtor, let's sign a contract. But God reminds me that the man who accepts my true type A outgoing personality is "always ready to be ready," protects me from potential disruptions because he does take his time, and he does love me enough to consider carefully everything we do as a couple, and ultimately as a family. I have learned to learn from him the rewards of patience and to consider his careful thought above the quickness of my own gut decision making.

Now, conversely, Frank has allowed himself to learn from me as well. Being a meticulous man in every sense, whether it was maintaining impeccable surroundings, personal care, clothing, finances, he was always pretty much on top of his game. That was one of the attributes I absolutely loved about him. He cared and still does about everything he touches and always puts his best foot forward. When we first got married, I wasn't as honest with him as it related to my finances. As a matter of fact, my finances were a mess. He didn't find out until we had been married for a while that I really was in poor financial shape. But he loved me, and God spoke to him through Ephesians 4:32 which says, "Be kind to each other, tenderhearted, forgiving one another, just as God through Christ has forgiven you." We went through a rocky time because of that, but Frank helped me, taught me, and was patient with me. He learned from me that you can love imperfection, and it is in that imperfection that strength rises and truth, even though hurtful, doesn't have to destroy a relationship. He was truly disappointed that I never let on that I was careless about money, but instead, he forgave me and loved me to the point of my getting whole and has never stopped.

As a couple, we've been extremely successful in allowing our individual selves to always be present. Our ying and yang habits have always made people admire us because we have always been that couple who is not afraid to be different, and yes, different to one another. You will hardly ever catch us dressing alike. That is something we just never did. And, just because one of us gets out of the bed and puts their right foot out first, has never meant that the other one would do the exact same thing. We have always taken pride in our own individuality, and there is no doubt that being bold in who we are individually has caused us to live this married life as unified as any couple who mirrors one another perfectly.

My mother always said, "For every pot, there is a cover." She was so correct in that saying. When we met years ago in college, there is no way either of us would have guessed that we would end up marrying one another. We were just friends. But, here's the most interesting thing about being "just friends," you learn the initial things about a person when you start off being their friend. You see their personality and what makes them tick. You observe their habits and can decide, even if you don't realize you're deciding, on whether or not you like them. As two individuals in this marriage, we have learned that our differences are exactly what attracts us to one another, for it is in our differences that we find a way to complete the package and make this union whole.

Some people have successful marriages, never going anywhere without the other person. I hear some couples who go to the grocery store together, who go to the coffee shop together, who go shopping together, and husbands who go to the nail shop with their wives not to get services, but just to be together. Trust us, that's wonderful if it works for them; it just would not be for us. And, that's ok.

If we were to give our most humble and servant advice to any couple contemplating marriage, it would be this: Know who you are first. Have a sense of your personality and make sure you encompass the good, the bad, and the ugly. When you know yourself, then you can freely learn the other person. That personality with whom you're interacting is not going to change, it will just get older. Differences can be beautiful if you both know how to take the needle, thread it, and weave it through your beautiful daily lives. You can create such beauty, and you can give one another devoted love, understanding, and warmth that we all crave and should have long-term. God puts us here to find that someone, that cover for our pot. It can be in the person who you least expect, but will find years of God-given love and happiness.

Conflict Resolution:
The Lachhu's

Hello, we're Dave and Sherrae Lachhu. We've been together for eleven years and married for eight years. Our story isn't the fairytale you grow up seeing on television or in the movies. It's one of both trials and triumphs. Most importantly, it's a story of love, acceptance, humility, and authentic living. Conflict is part of the human experience. Facing conflict within your marriage isn't only normal; it can also be a sign of a healthy marriage. It's our hope others might find inspiration in not only the love we show one another, but also in the hardships we've experienced and how we've managed to resolve them. "Consider it pure joy, my brothers and sisters, whenever you face trials of many kinds because you know that the testing of your faith produces perseverance." James 1:2-3 (NIV)

Cultural differences, disparities in communication styles, unique lived experiences, and just overall personality variations are contributing factors to how we both experience and resolve conflict within our relationship. We cohabitated for the first three years we were together prior to getting married. During that time, there were few arguments, and when we did have them, they were what we considered insignificant. The two-and-a-half years following our wedding, were some of the most challenging. It was as if we were on a constant emotional roller coaster of extremely high highs and devastatingly low lows. Truthfully, it was only through God's grace, prayer, our commitment to our marriage, self-reflection, dedication to authentic living, and our willingness to be vulnerable with ourselves and one another that we were able to make it through those years.

Dave says: I was raised in a culture where men dominate the women. Men are usually the primary breadwinners, and that also means they set the tone for how things should happen in their home and in the marriage. While this was always my feeling about marriage, when I met Sherrae, I presented as much more progressive in my ideals around gender roles and expectations. Sherrae was direct about what she wanted and what she didn't want in a partner and in a relationship. I would tell her I felt similarly, even though I didn't. I would often tell her what I thought she wanted to hear, instead of how I really felt. Later, I learned this was a huge mistake. Once we began experiencing conflict, I realized much of it was due to my lack of communication of my true feelings while acting out my emotions in a passive-aggressive manner. I would often do the bare minimum around the house, or not seek out possible employment or financial opportunities, because I felt I should be in control of the money.

Sherrae wanted me to oversee our finances, but that meant doing the work and being responsible in a way that felt burdensome at the time. Basically, I wanted the title and respect of overseeing our finances without doing the work. I would undermine her efforts, then claim ignorance or shutdown once called out. I realized that a lot of the mentality and behavior I had was not only from my upbringing, but also from my previous marriage. At some point, I realized if things were going to be different, I would need to be different. I recognized that Sherrae happened to be better in managing finances than I was, and it didn't mean I was any less of a man.

Once our marriage was nearly destroyed and we were on the verge of splitting, I realized I needed to take accountability for my behaviors if I wanted to see a change in my marriage. My decision to address and correct my mistrust of Sherrae's intentions was a big part of what led to my changed behavior. One of the things she taught me early in our relationship was the importance of reciprocity and accountability. Once I allowed God to show me my ways and ways in which I hurt Sherrae, I realized I was not reciprocating the trust and honesty she had shown me. I also failed to be accountable for my thoughts, words, and actions and would resort to being defensive or blaming when my actions were called out. Change was challenging, but it was worth it. As we both say, growth is painful but worth it.

Sherrae says: For me, after the devastation of my first marriage ending in divorce, I decided to improve as a person and as a wife so that my next relationship would be healthy. However, prior experiences made me hypervigilant, obsess over-finding errors in our marriage, and correcting them instead of learning to love the reality of my current imperfect union. In my desire to have a healthy marriage, I often placed unreal or unfair expectations on Dave and me. My intentions were earnest, but I believe it had a negative impact and led to increased conflict. I later learned that Dave felt the pressure of the expectation to only have positive experiences in our daily interactions.

Most challenging for me was the realization that everything Dave initially communicated to me about his desires regarding our relationship was untrue. It was hurtful, we didn't have enough trust between us for him to be honest and equally hurtful. He didn't give me a chance to make a choice to be with him based on honest information. It took a while to truly forgive him, as well as forgive myself for my unforgiveness and unfair expectations. It took years for either of us to realize how the dishonesty in the beginning affected our marriage, and just as many years to heal. It was a fragile and complex process. It took prayer, personal accountability, and even couples counseling to heal the trauma wounds experienced in the first few years of marriage. As patient and forgiving as my husband believed me to be, God showed me my rigidity in forgiving and moving forward. "Be kind and compassionate to one another, forgiving each other, just as in Christ God forgave you." Ephesians 4:32 (NIV)

There are several measures in addressing and resolving conflict in marriage. One is to pray that God will protect you, your mate, and your marriage; that he would guide your steps so that you both work for and not against your union. If either my husband or I win, then the marriage loses. Ask God to allow you to see yourself and your mate the way he sees you both. Frequently, when dealing with conflict in your marriage, we tend to only look at our perspective. We don't take the time to see things from our mate's perspective; neither do we give them the benefit of the doubt that their intentions may be good even when they've done something that seems unacceptable.

It is important to determine the underlying cause of conflict in your marriage. All arguments have themes. The goal is to determine what your arguments tend to focus on. Is it money, sex, kids, infidelity, family, role expectations? Whatever the ongoing theme in your argument is, requires working together to determine what the root cause is, because it is typically not what you think it's about. Common arguments are about sex and money, but that's often the superficial cause for the argument. The root cause is often a power struggle, unmet role expectations, or lack of trust. Once the cause is identified, work to address it when you're both in a place to hear from one another. This may be the time to enlist a marriage counselor so that you're both able to share with one another in a safe space.

In addition to the measures listed above, the following tips can assist couples in safeguarding their marriages from unhealthy conflict. Learn to develop empathy for one another. Set up ground rules for how to engage when you're upset with one another. It becomes problematic when couples attack one another or criticize the individual instead of focusing on the behavior that negatively impacts them. Don't allow your anger to take over, and don't remain angry. "My dear brothers and sisters, take note of this: Everyone should be quick to listen, slow to speak, and slow to become angry because human anger does not produce the righteousness that God desires" (James 1:19-20 NIV).

Be vulnerable enough to apologize when you're wrong; ask for forgiveness when needed and demonstrate the apology further through changed behavior. Conflict is resolved much easier when you've built up your love bank. "Love is patient, love is kind. It does not envy, it does not boast, it is not proud. It does not dishonor others, it is not self-seeking, it is not easily angered, it keeps no record of wrongs. Love does not delight in evil but rejoices with the truth. It always protects, always trusts, always hopes, always perseveres" (1 Corinthians 13:4-7 NIV).

It is our hope that each person reading this experiences a healthy, happy marriage with healthy conflict. We expect couples will takeaway useful nuggets from not just our lows, but also how we made it through those lows to the other side.

Generational Love:
The Johnson's

G od's Gift. Edward and I have been married forty-three years, and we have always believed we are soulmates. Before our wedding, my wise grandmother implored us to never go to bed angry because we would start each new day in the same rut. She also told us to always respect one another and honor our marriage vows. We promised her we would heed her advice, and with God's guidance, neither of us has ever broken that promise. Sometimes when people talk about finding their soulmate, they are describing someone who does everything the way they want it done and who acts the way they want them to act. That is not a soulmate, that is someone with an ulterior motive, a manipulator. They will say and do whatever it takes to eventually get their way.

A soulmate is a person who completes you, a missing puzzle piece. Someone, God has chosen for you who will be at your side through the ups and downs of life. Someone who loves you every day and never allows anyone or anything to come between you or threaten the wonderful gift of love God has given you both. You know this is your soulmate because you are a better person because of them, and even when you disagree, you always respect one another.

"Love is patient; love is kind. It does not envy; it does not boast; it is not proud. It does not dishonor others; it is not self-seeking; it is not easily angered; it keeps no record of wrongs" (Corinthians 13:4-5).

Humility Ed was drafted as a defensive end by the Cincinnati Bengals out of Southern Methodist University (SMU) in Dallas, but on the advice of a trusted coach, he decided to sign with the Detroit Wheels, a team in a new league. He saw me at a team party and later asked my best friend, Grace Hightower, for my number. She asked if it was okay, but I refused.

I was not interested in dating a jock. Shortly after, the league folded, and Ed returned home to Texas.

Several months later, Grace and another friend wanted to take a road trip to Texas, so they convinced me to call Ed. We didn't take the trip, but he and I talked almost every day over the next six months. We were married the next year. After our marriage, Ed had to decide if he would continue his current job or accept an offer to try out for the Cleveland Browns. He unselfishly put my desires before his and let me decide. I knew how much he wanted to give it one more try, so he went camping and stayed through the entire pre-season. Upon his return, we moved to Detroit, and he began working for General Motors, where he retired after thirty-six and-a-half years.

"Do nothing out of selfish ambition or vain conceit. Rather, in humility value others above yourselves, not looking to your own interests but each of you to the interests of the others.
Philippians 2:3-4 (NIV)

TRIALS

None of us can ever know when our faith will be tested. Ed and I married when I was twenty-six, and he was twenty-four, so we were ready to start our family immediately after moving to Detroit. Month after month passed until the months turned into years. We eventually went through the early stages of in-vitro fertilization to no avail. After six years of disappointment, tears, and despair, we decided we would adopt a child. We went through a wonderful place in Detroit called Homes for Black Children. They were very thorough in checking our background, and we were excited to hear about the many toddlers who were waiting for a family. We decided to wait until after our home visit to look at photos and learn more about the children before deciding. Our home visit was scheduled for the middle of February 1982, and we passed with flying colors.

The final requirement was our complete physicals, which were scheduled for the beginning of March 1982. Ed arrived at our doctor's office first, so he completed his examination. After my examination, our doctor looked at me and said, "Hold on a minute. Let me get Ed." I can't explain how nervous I was during those two or three minutes. I wondered, 'What in the world did he find?' As soon as Ed stepped into the room, our doctor began smiling and said, "You two are pregnant!" Our oldest daughter was born in November 1983, and we were advised if we wanted another child, we needed to wait no longer than a few years. Her sister was born almost two years later in November 1985.

Ed and I have told our story to dozens of young couples over the years who have longed for a child. Some were later blessed with a child through normal conception, some through in- vitro fertilization, and some opened their hearts and adopted. We believe the strength of your love and your faith can see you through any adversity. We are the living proof.

Isaiah 41:10 So, do not fear, for I am with you, do not be dismayed, for I am your God, I will strengthen you and help you; I will uphold you with my righteous right hand.

Roles and Responsibilities: The Witherspoon's

We are Eric & Laverne Witherspoon. Our most important question is: What are the Roles and Responsibilities in a marriage?

According to the Bible, Ephesians 5 commands wives to respect their husbands. How do we honor what the Bible has requested from us? As a couple, we must first realize if we are members of the body of Christ and we abide under the umbrella of obedience to Christ, we have to come to an understanding early in the relationship by identifying each other's roles and responsibilities.

Roles and responsibilities are safeguards from God. God encourages us to respect each other by revering, loving, and being truthful with each other, helping each other, valuing each other's characters, and being mindful and attentive to each other's needs. Within our relationship, we must both attend to each other's needs and pay close attention when one is being neglected.

We did not establish roles and responsibilities for this new union, causing essential areas of the family to be neglected. When roles and responsibilities are established within marriage, the couple realizes they are on the same winning team. In the book of Genesis, Chapter 1, the first thing God did after creating Adam and Eve in the Garden was to give them shared responsibilities. When we started delegating our roles and responsibilities, our children knew how the landscape of our family was set up, and they respected each parents' role even when they tried to cross over while being mad at either parent. Roles and responsibilities allowed us to find balance with our finances, quality time, receiving and giving gifts, our act of services, our physical touch, and with our words of affirmation, which is the five love languages in our lives.

Being two active duty soldiers, our initial roles and responsibilities that were established up front were switched during deployment. When my husband Eric deployed, I would have to switch roles and take on the role of being a financial manager of the household bills so that Eric's focus would be solely on his deployment and the care and safety of his soldiers. When I deployed, Eric would take on the role of taking care of the children, their schoolwork, and all household duties, including a financial manager. So, we have experienced a role and responsibility shift in the landscape of the family when circumstances change.

I remember when Eric became sick with cancer, everything that was established within our guidelines changed. Every role and responsibility pertaining to the family became my sole responsibility from being the caretaker of Eric, the financial manager, and the decision-maker for life and death questions in the event Eric did not survive. Shifting roles causes a breakdown in the marriage, not in a bad way but in a way that I was sometimes stretched beyond responsibilities that I could not carry or handle. This period became a dark period, and this was the period that I had to turn it all over to God.

As a blended family, there were things we both learned pertaining to our roles and responsibilities as husband and wife. Some of the lessons learned were not to incorporate old habits and failures, and therefore we both assumed shared duties to make the marriage work and not break it down. We realized that we may not have the same role and responsibilities as we had in our previous union. In our previous unions, both of our focus was outside of the household, for example, educational goals, establishing businesses and careers.

As we continued with our previous roles, there were certain important areas of the family dynamics that were neglected. We quickly realized that no one had taken on the responsibility of nurturing our children. Once this was made evident to us, we went back to the family table and regrouped in this landscape called marriage as we identified our roles that each of us would take on and be responsible for. One of the outcomes, among other things, I assumed the responsibility of nurturing our children while my husband Eric took on the role of being the breadwinner and the protector. This came with many sacrifices as I put my educational goals and careers on hold to make sure the children's needs and wants were attended to along with Eric's needs and wants.

As a married couple, we tried to establish our roles and responsibilities based on the Bible and our spiritual foundation. We fell back on responsibilities based on our culture and the way we understood them when we were kids, and by indulging in cultural roles and responsibilities within a marriage. Eric's role was primarily outside the house, while my roles were inside the house, as I demonstrated the qualities of a Proverbs 31 woman. I cooked, cleaned, and attended to the immediate needs of the children and Eric.

We realized that establishing roles and responsibilities following cultural norms did not work for our marriage. Some days we loved each other, and some days we could not stand each other, and at a period in our struggle, we found ourselves heading back to divorce court. We realized that we had to establish times when the spotlight had to be shifted from one to the other. We eventually shared the responsibilities together. If Eric saw that dishes needed to be washed after coming home, realizing that I had a long day with my responsibilities at home, he would pitch in and wash the dishes, sweep the floor, wash clothes, etc. I realized that Eric was out longer than a normal day, and the trash needed to be taken out, she would take it out and not wait for him to do it. This became a new norm of shared responsibilities within our marriage.

As a couple, we had to develop greater will power in listening to each other cry for love or cry for help. We had to be mature enough to know when to ask each other for help, which was extremely hard in the beginning of our relationship because we are two very strong-willed people. This was a responsibility that both had to take on. By taking on this role, we were both responsible for each other's pain and what to do in helping fix what was causing the pain. We realized that several things within the landscape of our relationship changed; we realized that by asking each other for help when we fell short, was showing each other that we trusted what we both brought to the marriage table. We trusted each other's personal experience, skills, insight, and opinion by making ourselves vulnerable to each other, and it was in that time of vulnerability that made us even stronger.

Spiritual leadership is one role that is an important value in our marriage. Philippians 2:4 (NIV) says, "Look not every man on his own things, but every man also on the things of others." As tension builds in many marriages, our marriage was not any different. This was true for me and Eric in our early years of marriage. When we first got together, I am sure Eric thought, "Oh my, I am marrying a Bishop's daughter," and believed he would have to act a certain way around my dad.

Fortunately, Eric liked the way I was as a Christian woman, with the morals, values, and standards that I lived by; so eventually Eric allowed me to lead the family spiritually in the early years of our marriage. After accepting Christ as his personal savior and several talks amongst ourselves, we felt that the man should be the one to lead the family spiritually if we were to live according to the scriptures. Eventually, we made the decision that Eric would take the spiritual role in leading our family, making him not only our Mandingo Warrior but also the Spiritual Warrior.

One of the final responsibilities that we placed on ourselves as a married couple was to be a living example for our children; we wanted them to see what marriage should look like and understand that marriage is not always perfect. We wanted our children to understand the importance of identifying responsibilities in rich marriage whether they are individually or shared between both. We wanted them to realize that both partners in the marriage is responsible for holding each other accountable. We emphasized that always having open and honest communication is one of the essential elements of a successful and happy marriage.

"And now these three remain: faith, hope, and love. But the greatest of these is love"
(1 Corinthians 13:13 NIV).

If you want to leave a rich legacy for your children as far as marriage is concerned, remember love is a choice, and in choosing the one that you would like to spend your life with, make a conscious decision to show your children how to establish roles and responsibilities in a marriage, to make it a healthy relationship.

BLENDED FAMILIA: THE ROJAS'

Picture this America, the summer of 2000, a young African American single mother living in southwestern Pennsylvania, out on the town with my sister at salsa dance classmates. I go to one of the many spots in town that provided live Latin bands or Latin DJs. While I am learning to perfect my steps, I get up the courage to approach a guy across the room who appeared to have a friendly face. The guy who had just clocked out from his shift at a local restaurant, had come to America to have a better life and forget the disappointment he had experienced prior to crossing the border from Mexico. I approached the guy and asked him to dance, which was the beginning of our story.

Our story, my husband and I, two people from two different countries, two different cultures, that spoke two different languages but met on common ground through music and dance. My husband came from a small town about thirty minutes outside of Mexico City and had come to America after experiencing heartbreak when his long-time girlfriend ended their relationship. He came to America not only for the American Dream, but also to find love and security. A family of his own is what his heart had desired for as long as he could remember. His journey here was dangerous and difficult because he had come through illegal channels, but God's hand had protected and covered him, even though he hadn't followed the law of the land. God's grace and mercy kept him right up to the faithful night he met me.

As for me, I was a young woman who was a single mother. Although I was a native to the area we both were residing in, I also experienced pain in previous relationships. God's grace and mercy had kept me throughout my dating and life's journey. Because I had a child from one of my former relationships, I desired a family of my own and a partner that would love my child as his own. I, too, wanted to feel secure and loved. Though we didn't have the words to communicate, we believe God's hand was in our story of blending from beginning to the end.

The interesting thing about blending your family is that it's the great equalizer. If you think about it, whether you are the one with the child or both bring children into the relationship, there are new experiences, rules, and expectations on the horizon. Everyone has to learn a new normal. My husband, and I were not aware of what we were about to undertake. I, as the biological parent, when I think back now, I know I underestimated the level of humility and courage it would take for me to hear the hard things from our daughter as we entered into our marriage covenant.

My husband became "Papi" to our daughter, Ashley. One moment came to mind when my daughter and I were cleaning up after dinner in the kitchen. My husband and our first-born child, Felipe Josue, were in the living room playing on the floor. My daughter turns to me and asks, "Mom, can I ask you something?" Me doing the routine mom thing, cleaning, and somewhat listening, heard her ask, "Am I your rough draft?" My heart dropped, and I felt a brief panic come over me. That was the most vulnerable and naked I had ever felt in my role in our new family life. Our daughter had recognized the inequity of my parenting compared to her childhood. No matter how much I tried to mask my imperfections from my past by including my daughter in every activity in the present, I had to be open to hear her heart and understand the truth of her experience. The Holy Spirit provided the words at that moment. My answer was "Yes, yes. You were my rough draft."

I needed to confess my faults as James instructs so that we could both be healed of the damage of my past ignorance and begin the work on building a safe home for everyone, where each person can be heard. In the bible James 5:16 says, "Therefore, confess your sins to each other and pray for each other so that you may be healed. The prayers of a righteous person are powerful and effective (NIV)." These words of wisdom were meant for parenting and are tools for those in blended families to alleviate the fear of anyone feeling left out. Blending a family and keeping the family together takes a level of humility and openness; with the help of the Lord it can be a forever family. Choosing to answer my daughter's tough question instead of avoiding it, helped all three of us, my daughter, my husband, and me, with learning how to communicate the hard things. It also provided me an opportunity to apologize to our daughter.

One of my Felipe's greatest challenges was trying to learn to build trust with us while growing trust with me in a different area of our home life, "parenting." My husband and I had never lived together until we were married and said, I do. He was Mr. Phillip to my daughter, and then he became an instant father to a preteen child. The level of pressure he felt trying not to fail our daughter or me in the beginning years, came out as frustration. There were many days where we did not agree on a choice of when to discipline, but we both knew that for him to be respected and become comfortable in his role as "Papi," I needed to step back. His biggest fear was to hear the words, "You are not my father." Early on, he would always communicate that he was not trying to replace her father. His goal was to reassure her that he respected her relationship with her biological father. Her biological father was her father, but she would always be his daughter, not his stepdaughter. The bible talks about words having the power of life and death in Proverbs 18:21 which states, "The tongue has the power of life and death, and those who love it will eat its fruit." The words of my husband publicly stating my daughter is his daughter and giving her space to choose her name for him, opened both of their hearts. The fruit of those words of endearment, "daughter" and "Papi," was the fertilizer for their relationship. We believe in such a powerful way. Just as I was his forever partner until death do us part, those vows were for their relationship as father and daughter, as well.

We want you to know that your words have the power to change the growth and strength of your family as you bond. A simple declaration of your position as mom or dad and not stepmom or stepdad, changes the trajectory of family relationships. There are times when we talk and think how different my husband and our daughter's relationship would be if he were Mr. Phillip and not "Papi." How that would impact her siblings? How would it impact our marriage?

There are so many complexities in family life. When you add the experience of blending families, it truly takes a cord of three strands to passionately, lovingly, and patiently keep your family on the best course. God has planned for you as a unit. We want to leave you with knowing that if God can take our situations with all the challenges of culture and language, and blend our family into this unit, fortified by our belief in Jesus Christ, He can do the same for you and your family. Blending your family is a journey, not a destination. When times are challenging, ask yourself, "Are you operating from a place of humility with your spouse and children? What language are you using when communicating? Are your words loving? Are you the stepchild's Papi or Mami in word or action?"

Matthew 19:26 states, "Jesus looked at them and said, 'With man, this is impossible, but with God, all things are possible.'"

Love That Works:
The Hoskins'

We are Paul and Michele Hoskins and we met at the beginning of our corporate careers and have been happily married for twenty-nine years. Paul and I are serial entrepreneurs, proud parents of twins, and reside in San Antonio Texas. Michele and my dedication to Jesus Christ is evident in the areas of ministry, business, and community service they have committed to over the years.

We are often asked, "How is it working with your spouse? How do you handle being together all the time?" As entrepreneurs and co-laborers in ministry, we have put ourselves at significant risk by being on the same pay schedule, working in the same industry, sharing the same office, workload, and financial responsibilities. We have reduced the income inequality in our household and created an enjoyable proprietorship business structure. We both have skill sets that complement the business. Most importantly, the level of respect we have for each other's professional skills denotes that "Love That Works, Works!"

Very few spouses are afforded the honor of working with the person they love most! Love That Works, makes the daily commute to the office more exciting. Love That Works, promotes togetherness. Togetherness and the thought of working twenty-four hours a day, seven days a week, three hundred sixty-five days a year, sounds sexy, right? Even better, holding hands while driving to the office, meeting for lunch to share a cup of soup, or for a mid-afternoon rendezvous is very exciting and romantic. In reality, running a business or serving together in ministry is romantic, too, and will challenge even the strongest marriage in unimaginable ways. Statistics suggest that entrepreneurial couples have a higher rate of divorce than other married people; approximately 43 to 48 percent. To avoid becoming a statistic, God is first in our marriage! We strive to live according to His word, which provides the principles needed for a Love That Works (Genesis 2:18-25, NIV).

Our primary focus is to have fun, create memorable moments, teach our children entrepreneurship, and build generational wealth. We believe that faith and finance can coexist. Entrepreneurship is an interesting profession synonymous with challenges and opportunities. Even though we do not have the comfort of a corporate job or income, we trust God, have followed our passion, and enjoy the freedom of controlling our destiny. God has given us talents and allowed us to create a shared business model of success (Psalms 37:4, NIV). We live our motto, Love That Works, Works because we love the nature of our work. Even though we may work 10 to 12 hour-days, seventy or more hours a week, creatively, together, we solve problems and make life better for others. We are blessed to serve others through community outreach, the creation of job opportunities, and college scholarships. Our business offers products and services for the public, non-profits, schools, and corporations to enjoy. These things are contributors to our authentic message, Love That Works, Works!

Love That Works, takes work. As individuals, we work hard to maintain our authenticity. Morning hair bonnets, torn tee-shirts, baggy shorts, and ashy knees on the twenty-step walk from the bathroom to the office is just one way we maintain authenticity as we work together. We have put perfection into perspective. We believe that it doesn't have to be perfect to be good and refuse to succumb to worldly assumptions. We realized early in our marriage, we don't have to look great and be perfect all day every day to have a solid marriage. We don't give attention to our imperfections, and neither should you. Imperfections help us all to become the best version of our authentic self. Becoming the best version of yourself means living for yourself and not for others. This requires learning to say no to things that don't please you, doing more of the things that bring you joy, without the influence of others.

We love to travel and have dined in the best restaurants. One time against our better judgment, we went on vacation with some friends. The husband and wife we traveled with got in a fight and fought the entire vacation. Good thing, we had separate hotel rooms. This vacation allowed us to see our friends at their best and their worst. Our friends were loafers. Every morning we had to gauge how long it would be before they would be ready to go. One morning we waited for one hour in a restaurant for them to join us for breakfast. We ate without them and went on a tour without them. This vacation caused us to stress because they were stressed and diminished the quality of our vacation. The lesson learned; a great vacation is about being around the right people, doing what you want to do when you want. To maintain a Love That Works, we travel with our children and parents to create our own fun and family memories.

Love That Works laughs. We often laugh about the time we were in the car having heated fellowship, and Paul wouldn't end this very long conversation. To get him to stop, I turned on Paul's heated seats. As I looked out the window, chuckling to myself, Paul began sweating profusely on a 100-degree day. Paul thought he was getting sick, with a fever, and turned the air conditioner up high. Just to find out 10 minutes later, instead of arguing, I had turned on the heated seats to end the conversation. Guess what? It worked. We laugh about the time Paul drove the twins to school, 45 minutes away from home, only to discover when our son got out of the car, he didn't have on shoes. We laughed about the call my wife received from Barak Obama on her cell phone, and she hung up because she thought the call was a prank. Fortunately, the then-Senator Obama called back and told us something personal, and we knew it was really him. The best laugh we shared is when we became entrepreneurs. We had worked ten, 14-hour days straight and overslept on the fifteenth day. After we turned the alarm off, we looked at each other and said, "We are late. Guess what? We are the bosses and can't get fired!" We laugh daily at the funny things our children say. We laugh with our children and believe that we are creating a healthy marriage template for our children to follow.

Love That Works, models a healthy relationship for our children. We refuse to become complacent in our parenting roles. Complacency can contribute to co-dependence, which is not the relationship model we want our children to learn. We do not put the children first, at the expense of the marriage. Modeling a Christ-like marriage indicates balance in remaining lined up to serve God first, the marriage, children, family, friends, and the business. There is nothing more hurtful than missing out on a life event due to a lack of balance. Even the most skilled and organized couples cannot anticipate daily challenges and interruptions. Thus, commitment to maintaining balance is critical to a Love That Works.

Love That Works, works on commitment, communication, and connection. The spouses of entrepreneurs most commonly ask for a divorce because of neglect. We commit to a Love That Works, by doing whatever it takes spiritually, emotionally, physically, financially, and personally to make the marriage work. This doesn't mean that one spouse can always have their way, but is a moral commitment to keep the marriage intact.

We communicate by taking advantage of every opportunity to talk, text, and show our true feelings. Ensuring that we know, feel, and understand how important each of us is to the marriage, family, and business, confirms our relationship remains connected and healthy. Love That Works, works on remaining connected. Life can get crazy, making it difficult to connect sometimes. We no longer let activities outside the home control our schedules. We have let go of things that control our ability to connect. We connect by putting electronics in time out - no cell phones or technology at the dinner table, and cell phones are off by 8:00 pm, except for business or family calls. We connect when one cooks, the other cleans the kitchen. We connect by sharing responsibilities for raising our children. We connect through fasting, worship, and prayer. We don't let unimportant things interfere with our connection. Love That Works, connects by expressing gratitude for every blessing God has provided. We connect on date night, or when we stay up all night watching movies. We connect affectionately and playfully so that our children can see the many ways Love That Works, works.

Love That Works, works on handling issues of the heart and mind that could damage the marriage, family, or business. Love That Works, works on being irreplaceable and different. Yet, special. Love That Works, works to increase spiritual hydration and maintain each other's well-being. Love That Works, works hard knowing that no matter how successful we become in business or ministry, we must always seek to be shining examples of God's love and provisions.

God's love is a love that works. Can you commit to practicing one act of love every day and watch Love That Works, Work?

MARRIAGE AFTER DIVORCE: THE BROWN'S

Imagine embarking on a new journey, and you pack your bags that include your toothbrush and toothpaste, check, shoes, check, clothes, check, passport, check. So, you're excited, and you step up to the ticket counter only to be told your bags are too heavy. You have reached the maximum weight allowed to travel on this journey. Now you need to unpack your bags while the whole line stares at you while you fumble through the items in your bags, deciding what things you don't need on this journey, and you begin discarding non-essential items to lighten the load.

We are Ken and Derschaun Brown, and we have been married four years, we were both married to someone else. Suddenly, our present marriage began to feel heavy at times, and we couldn't shake it. After having a few hard conversations, we came to realize the problem was not us alone. It was the baggage we brought from our past experiences, our parents, and our previous marriages.

When Ken and I remarried, we both brought unhealthy relationship patterns and uber trust issues from our first marriage, which almost sabotaged our new union before we got it off the ground. Those issues stemmed from my childhood trauma of being abandoned by my father. If in and out was a parenting style, it would be his. Our relationship was very inconsistent, which made me feel invaluable, not worthy, unimportant, which caused me Derschaun to be very guarded and frankly, not trusting. Unconsciously, I took that pain into my first marriage, and because I didn't deal with it, the cycle repeated itself. There I was again hurt, abandoned, and unable to trust.

On the other hand, my lack of trust stemmed from when I was ten years old, and my father and mother decided to get divorced. As a ten-year-old boy, like most children, I was still in my formative years. My world views were being shaped and formed. My foundation was shattered, and my home was broken. Frequently, we are either running to something or from something. Instead of running to a successful marriage, I was running from ever having to go through a divorce because of the pain my family and I experienced. As a man, I never wanted to experience that pain again, let alone have my wife and children experience that pain and trauma. Unconsciously, in lieu of spending time and energy on building to win, my underlining goal was to work on not losing. Hence, I found myself playing not to lose instead of playing to win. I am reminded of Job when he said, "For the thing, I greatly feared has come upon me, and what

I dreaded has happened to me." Job 3:25 (NIV). After being married eighteen years, my marriage abruptly ended, and I was left asking questions like who, what, when, and how did this happen? Unconsciously I brought that same pain into our marriage, and once again, the cycle repeated itself.

The hardest part about these bags is that neither of us could recognize their weight. We chalked it up to "these were our real feelings and how we were raised, and if you love me, you will accept all of me." Believe it or not, no matter how much we prayed, cried, or danced around them, or went as far as to not even talk about them at all, our bags did not and could not unpack themselves or disappear. How do you unpack something that you aren't fully aware is there? How do you let go of something that you don't realize is weighing you down? Until we recognized that our bags were real problems, we couldn't unpack them. We would often get so close, and suddenly, the pain of our past filled our hearts and minds because those "invisible cousins; fear, doubt, and worry" were in our bags, but we couldn't see them. Some days we even doubted that it was worth it or worth fighting for.

Once we finally identified and acknowledged that these cousins or feelings existed and were real, we committed to always working on defeating those cousins, because if we didn't, we would allow them to rob us of our marriage. We discovered that if you don't trust yourself and your feelings, you'll never open up. We found that the last time we trusted and were open and vulnerable to a spouse, we were betrayed, hurt, and ended in divorce. We understand as long as we continued to live in the shadows of the fear of rejection and abandonment, our thoughts will trap us, and we will never get past our past. We have now discovered that if we don't trust ourselves and come clean about our feelings, we will never open up. We had to trust each other enough to be open and be vulnerable. As the word reminds us, "The thief cometh not, but for to steal, and to kill, and to destroy: I am come that they might have life, and that they might have it more abundantly" (John 10:10). To experience that abundant life in our marriage, we had to develop and commit to operating off a new flight plan. "Therefore, if anyone is in Christ, he is a new creation; old things have passed away and behold all things are becoming new" (2 Corinthians 5:17 NIV).

Our NEW flight plan consists of:

- ✪ Keeping Christ at the head of our marriage
- ✪ Loving each other as if we've never been hurt before. It's not always easy, but with Christ all things are possible
- ✪ As long as we remember that our partner is not a problem, but the problem is the problem. Attack the problem together and not my partner.
- ✪ Please don't spend time trying to interpret your partner's feelings and support them.
- ✪ Be quick to listen and slow to speak.
- ✪ Stay out of your feelings and allow your actions to lead freely.

✪ Control and manage the conditions of your heart. This enables those cousins/feelings to remain defeated and powerless to creep back in.

Let's be real, some events can change everything about you and your family for the rest of your life. Whether it's a loss, a betrayal, or infidelity. Without a doubt, those things affect the dynamics of our relationships. Before you decide to take that journey together, whether it's the

first time or like us, the second time around, it's critical that you unpack your bags and remember, don't let fear, doubt and worry creep in. Getting hurt is a part of life. It's inevitable. But, it's not the end of the story. God creates all things new. Because the times and seasons that fear, doubt, and worry are absent from our marriage and mind, it's magical. The more we began to understand that "There is no fear in love, but perfect love casts out fear. Fear has to do with punishment, and whosoever fears has not been perfected in love" (1 John 4:18).

Marriage & Diversity: The Higby's

Christ, the epitome of love, the demander of diversity, and the advocate for the least of these, is the central figure and foundation for Ricky & Naomi, otherwise known as RkyXnao. This is our story, a story of a widower father of two young girls and a divorcee mother of a teenage boy. A story wrought with quiet confidence, disagreements, beauty, misunderstandings, a wonderful smile, angst, iced tea, dog parks, powder-blue Chuck Taylor sneakers, "Jesus"

shoes, and a mutual focus to enable the best in others.

In January 2015, I experienced a "chance encounter" at a mutual friend's home with a handsome man who had perfectly coiffed hair and wore Jesus-like sandals. I was quite intrigued by him, as all the men sat in front of the television glued to the football game, this peculiar man was more content talking about the ins and outs of creating the perfect ballet hair bun for his daughter with me and the other women. I always looked at our "chance" meeting as a "God thing." I had been invited to our friend's home several times, but being a bit of an introvert who tends to shy away from crowds, my typical response was a most appreciative declination to most invitations. This time was a bit different; I felt compelled to go.

That happened to be the day that, what is now our blended family, met for the first time. Soon thereafter, Ricky invited me to meet him at Montgomery's Vaughn Park. Let me clarify, his youngest daughter, Ella, called to beg me to meet them at the park. How could I say no? This would be considered our first "date" and was by far the most unusual first date either of us had ever been on. Ella had quite a few hard-pressing questions for me in her attempt to "figure me out." I was just as smitten with this child, as I was becoming with her father. To be quite honest, I was scared to death, and every part of my brain was thinking, "I am not so sure about any of this."

I was almost forty years old and had been single long enough to not rush into anything that did not feel right and meet very specific criteria. This good-looking man with perfect posture, and Jesus sandals was not exactly showing up with everything I had strategically placed on my vision board for the man I would spend the rest of my life with. Sure, he seemed like a great guy who loved God, loved his kids, seemed safe and trustworthy, in an innocent kind of way, but on the other hand, I had a lot of reservations about literally everything else regarding this relationship.

I had always prayed for daughters, but was I ready to be a full-time mother of two grieving girls? Would they resent me? How would my son feel about this budding relationship? Was I ready to give up my peaceful, quiet life? My mother will most certainly think I have gone mad. Would we ever have time to date and get to know each other without children around watching our every move and listening in on our every conversation? It sounds crazy, but yes, all these thoughts and many more were racing through my mind, on date number one! ...Oh, and what is up with the Jesus sandals?

For me, Ricky, it was much less complicated. It was quite simple. Andy Mineo summed it up nicely in his song, "Lay up," where it states, "Should I marry my girl? [Is] she fly? [Does she] love God? She got a good mind? Oh boy, that's a layup!" That was all the confirmation I needed! On a bench in that same Vaughn Park, I asked for her hand, followed by a covenant ceremony soon thereafter, in a small garden along the water in Prattville, Alabama.

From the start, we were focused, at least in word, on following what Christ says as documented by Saints Mathew and Mark, that man and woman are no longer two, but one flesh and what God has joined, let no man separate. Coupling that with Saint Paul's direction to the Ephesian followers of "The Way," to selflessly give myself to her and for her to support me.

Our marriage has not at all been the standard boy meets girl, fall in love, get married, and live happily ever after. Blending our family was and is one of the biggest challenges we have ever had. Our marriage has had more ups and stomach-dropping falls than even the wildest roller coaster ride. Even as our goal is to exemplify Jesus, differences, SIGNIFICANT differences, still arose. Our seventeen-year-old son was not at all happy with any of these life changes. Our daughters struggled in their own way, as well. "Who is this lady who dad likes so much, and why is she changing our house and making us eat quinoa and throw away all the sugar cereal?"

We are opposites in every possible area, I repeat, every possible area. Not only in skin color, ethnicity, and heritage, but every preference from ice cream to favorite colors to TV shows. We personified ying and yang, fire and ice. Naomi's focus is practicality, mine is aesthetics. She prefers spicy, organic, and non-genetically modified. I like food from a box. She enjoys tousled and messy; whereas, I prefer straight, neat, and tidy. She likes things quiet and peaceful; for me, the louder and more chaotic, the better. We would be remiss not to mention all the cultural and personality differences we have, from music, food, and leisure, to police run-ins, and racial profiling.

I am a wild and crazy, curly-haired free spirit, who longs to have the warmth of the sun on my face as I sit and ponder, while Ricky spends most of his leisure time studying educational, theological & philosophical theory. I prefer to be in the moment, Ricky prefers to utilize every moment to maximum productivity, scheduling potty breaks somewhere in between. In the family, she is all about relationship, and he is laser-focused on function. These differences, however challenging, are a wonderful thing.

Difference is good, actually great, as all are created to do very specific things, and when that is capitalized on, beautiful things can happen, which we truly believe. This began to come alive as we discovered a new appreciation for cultural and ethnic differences. Our relationship was also the beginning of Ricky's education in satin pillowcases for naturally curly hair and the sad disparity in treatment according to race, of which he never realized until this beautiful wedded union of cultures.

Being in our culturally blended marriage is amazing and quite a privilege. We get to challenge the cultural status quo every single day. Jesus said, as recorded by Saint Paul, there is neither Jew nor Gentile, slave nor free, male nor female, for you are all one in Christ Jesus, again I repeat, one in Christ. As our focus is Christ, we have a unique opportunity to live out this verse and be a catalyst for perspective and culture change.

As a result of our diverse marriage, we realize there are two things in relation to oneness. First, there is an entirely different world out there, of which we knew nothing about it. Secondly, we cannot do marriage and family under our power. I, Ricky, am too selfish, prideful, and critical.

I, Naomi, am too independent and finicky to walk this marriage adventure on my own. We rely on the mantra "I cannot, but You [Jesus] can," while following Saint Paul's guidance to be kind, compassionate, and forgiving, and Jesus' beckoning to be gentle and humble as He is. We also came to rely heavily on community, unfettered communication, and mentorship to see what we are unable to see on our own.

That single, white, father of two, with his perfectly coiffed hair and Jesus-like sandals observed this tall, gorgeous, caramel-skinned mother of one walking across Vaughn Park in her powder-blue shirt and matching Chuck Taylor sneakers. A "chance encounter" created a dynamic relationship of pain and loss, give and take, patience and temper, ultimately a relationship of selfless love. Our mission is to encourage diversity in thought, to seek out, welcome, and engage in this diversity to build healthy relationships with a respect for and celebration of differences, to enable the best version of you and your mate.

Philippians 4:8 (NIV) "Finally, brethren, whatsoever things are true, honest, just, pure, lovely, of good report; if there be any virtue, and if there be any praise, think on these things."

Relationships of oneness come to fruition when we focus on what is "virtuous." When we understand and respect that we are ALL image-bearers of the Creator. Diversity in thought is a great thing, may we embrace it. We challenge you to know, expect, learn about, and rejoice in your mate's different perspective and experience. With intentionality about the diversity in your marriage, comes growth and oneness.

FRIENDS AND FAMILY:
THE RILEY'S

"*Love* is patient, **love** is kind. It does not envy; it does not boast; it is not proud. It is not rude; it is not self-seeking; it is not easily angered and keeps no record of wrongs. *Love* does not delight in evil but rejoices with the truth"

(1 Corinthians 13:1, NIV)

Friends Becoming Family through Love, Faith and Trusting God

From friendship to family. How does that work? By using the bible, which is the "inspired" holy word of God as the primary source for all of your family life decisions. The bible is never changing and all encompassing; it should be the primary source and resource for all healthy and successful relationships. Love, Faith and Trust in God are just a few of the godly principles and an example of how Jesus cultivated relationships with the twelve disciples. He taught them by being a living example and the epitome of Love, Faith, and Trust in God.

Our Story

I am Rev. Warren Riley, a licensed and ordained Minister, married to Zina; and we are both certified marriage coaches through Prepare and Enrich. Thirty-three years ago, we began our covenant journey with each other; God and clergy; all witnessed in front of over 350 family and friends.

Our story is truly one of love, trust, commitment, and faith. In our marriage, God is in the center and family is in our inner circle of love. We describe this as "*Warren and Zina's Loving God Circle.*"

TWO BECOMING ONE

We met as children when we were eleven and ten years old. Who knew Gods' fingerprints were already on us and our destiny was sealed in love, instantly we became friends. As teenagers, we did everything together; high school dances, skating, movies, bowling and a few times, we went on double dates together. The older we got, the closer we became. Our families were extremely close and viewed us as siblings because we were inseparable; our friends learned to love both of us, as we were a package deal. You could not befriend one without befriending the other.

During our seven years of hanging out, we finally acknowledged our attraction to each other, and started dating. Initially, our family members were a little surprised because everyone viewed us as brother and sister, not as a couple. We anticipated that it would be shocking to our siblings, and in time, people would realize that we were destined for each other. Our friendship, fellowship, and relationship were all grown from love and respect for one another. It was as if we each found the other part of ourselves in one another.

Warren enlisted in the Air Force, January of 1986, his first assignment was Alamogordo, New Mexico. While he was in Alamogordo, we were in constant contact. We wrote letters to each other daily and spoke on the phone when we could (this was before the internet). Although we were thousands of miles apart, we knew that the foundation of our relationship was our friendship. While he was in New Mexico, we worked daily to maintain that friendship. For Warren, living in Alamogordo, New Mexico was a HUGE culture shock! What was a young black man from Chicago to do in New Mexico? Grow up quickly and learn how to be successful in this new life. He had to be equipped with the proper survival tools to make all things possible.

During one of Warren's many trips back to Chicago, we became engaged. God knew that we did not want to live in New Mexico, but He always has a plan. A couple of months before our wedding day, we received the best wedding gift ever, an assignment to Italy. We were excited, poor, and had never been out of the country. That is when faith, love, and trust in God overcame all fears and anxieties of the unknown. We decided whatever God had in store for us in Italy, was better than our plans for New Mexico.

We arrived in Italy September 1987, just two young adults that had never left the United States. We were all alone in a foreign country; all we had was each other. God allowed us to believe that we were alone as He continued to work in the background of our lives. This move drew us closer together as we ventured out to start our new lives as husband and wife.

God placed five couples in our lives that we latched onto, and within three months of being in Italy, our friendships developed into family. We missed our family, but we were glad to meet couples with similar interests, morals, and the same family values. Our home became a hub of lifelong friendships. Our place was the hangout for all of our married and single friends. We ate, partied, and cried together during both difficult and joyous times. Most importantly, we grew in our love and relationships together. God was constantly at work in our lives.

From Italy, we moved to K.I. Sawyer Air Force Base, Michigan. God moved us to another place where we felt there was no support, but He remained in the background. As we began to settle into our new home and new life, we also began to meet new people who became lifelong friends. One of the couples became very active in church, and God became the center of their life. God strategically places people in your life as a guide if only for a season. According to the Blue Letter

Bible (BLB) BLOG, *God uses ordinary people in extraordinary ways!* God used friendship to plant the seed of attending church to strengthen our Love, Faith, and Trust in Him.

Every placed we lived while in the Air Force, we found couples to grow and fellowship with by getting out and meeting people. We went to church with these couples and spent many late nights laughing and crying. Our children grew up together and those friendships continue to be some of the most meaningful friendships we have ever formed, even to this day. Because we were separated from our biological family for twenty years, God placed those couples in our lives to act as our surrogate family. Our children call our friends "aunt" and "uncle" because that is who they were to our children and their children referred to us the same way. It was our Love, Faith, and Trust in God and each other that developed our friendships.

During our thirty-three years of marriage, whether we were together or in separate locations, we always made time for each other. While Warren was deployed, we made sure to speak on the phone as often as we could. Early in our relationship, we wrote letters to each other to stay connected while we were apart. When we were in the same place, we made sure to go on dates at least once a month, despite having children. We made sure to take time for our relationship to ensure that we grew together as a couple and not apart. Every night we would have dinner together to talk about our day. Communication was key in our success whether we were together or apart.

Our friendship is what has kept our relationship strong and is a major reason why we have multiple date nights each week. We want to keep the relationship ongoing because we realize we have to continue to dress up, go out on dates, and create new memories together. Always remember just because you are married, doesn't mean you can stop dating. You have to step up your dating game; whatever you did before your marriage is the same thing you have to continue to do.

As married people, we must be intentional about seeking out like-minded married couples and encourage one another on the importance of building friendships with our partners. Friendship is one of the two elements that really helped us understand that two is better than one.

The second element is spending time. Our families taught us the importance of developing relationships with one another. We were taught that a family must stay together because that's all you have. In order to keep the strong family bond, you must spend time together. We make it a priority to spend time with our friends and family. We often go on vacation with our children, sisters and mother. Every Sunday at our home is family day. We attend church in the morning and have great fellowship with dinner and game night in the evening. We were both raised in homes where family time was a priority. The importance of spending time together was instilled in us as children, and we have raised our children with same family values. Spending time together has only strengthened our bond, not only as a married couple, but as friends.

What God has joined is meant to be forever!

Remote Love:
The Pope's

W e are Johnnie and Chanel Pope, affectionately known as "The Popes." We are both retired military veterans that currently reside in San Antonio, Texas. We have been in a relationship with one another for a total of ten years and have been married four years. We chose to share on the topic, "Remote Love," because many individuals that are seriously dating or considering marriage operate under a false narrative, which ultimately suggests that long-distance relationships are doomed to fail. We believe that our personal story of long-distance love will increase insight, instill hope, and inspire others as they pursue courtship or marriage.

Together, we share forty-nine years of life experience and military expertise. As two former senior military leaders, Fortune-500 industry professionals, business owners, and parents of two adult children, we have lived and learned several significant life lessons concerning courtship and marriage. Therefore, we believe that sharing authentic life experiences is what truly helps others to realize that they can successfully master and overcome relationship challenges. Couples must be honest and vulnerable enough to admit to others that "perfection" truly does not exist in marriage or courtship; only the capacity for one to whole-heartedly do his or her very best to honor God and their mates. So, we decided to utilize our personal experiences, both good and bad, to help others succeed in relationships. Our hope is that our transparency will help other couples to face their fears, to avoid certain relationship pitfalls, and to believe that all things are possible with God.

THE BACK STORY

Our love story began remotely; in other words, it was a typical long-distance relationship. Before dating, we were acquainted with one another thirteen years earlier as teenagers in 1985. We lived in the same hometown growing up. However, as the years passed, memories of that acquaintance subtly faded. Interestingly, we were no longer familiar with one another when our paths suddenly crossed again thirteen years later. We did not remember one another.

My husband, Johnnie, had moved back to our hometown, and we quickly rekindled a promising friendship. At the time, he lived in Southeastern Virginia, and I lived in Central Texas. In 2011, I invited Johnnie to my doctoral graduation. After spending an adventurous and romantic weekend together, we established such a deep connection that we quickly decided to date one another, despite living 1,532 miles away. This blissful and euphoric honeymoon period led to several cross-country weekend excursions, thousands of hours on the phone, and ultimately the decision to become exclusive.

BARRIERS AND CHALLENGES

Let's say it definitely was not an easy journey! In this phase, both parties hit the pause button on the remote control and mutually stalled the Harlequin romance. The euphoria had somewhat faded, and now real-life began. One of the biggest challenges Johnnie and I both faced was effectively managing "work-life-balance." We both had difficulty finding the time to be physically present and emotionally available.

During a four-year period, from 2011 to 2015, Chanel and I endured tremendous life-stressors. I suddenly lost my brother in a tragic car accident. I was charged to assist my aging parents with serious medical challenges. I struggled to rebuild my insurance business, co-parented my children from a previous marriage that routinely presented relational challenges, and was forced to quickly adjust to retirement life after a twenty-five-year military career.

As Johnnie's partner I, also endured a significant amount of social stressors during this season of life.

I abruptly lost my beloved grandmother, grappled with being in a city without relatives or extended family, and was diagnosed with a severe chronic pain disorder. In addition, I endured covert racism and marginalization from my military leaders, and I was also forced to quickly adjust to retirement life after a twenty-four-year military career; with limited resources to aid in with that transition.

The totality of these significant life events, eventually took an emotional toll on us both. The emotional weight of it all forced us both to stop and address the elephant in the room. We had to face the hard truth that we were both "stressed out," and then realized that neither of us were to blame. Now, we had a choice to make. We had to decide if we would face our challenges head-on together or if we would avoid the intense emotional work and retreat. Retreating and emotional avoidance is always the easy way out initially, but in the long-run, it will cost you long-term connection and emotional intimacy.

After many heartfelt conversations, we ultimately decided our relationship was worth fighting for. We began to lean more heavily on our faith by consistently consulting God concerning the growth of our relationship. Prayer quickly became a routine practice and has remained a constant staple at the core of our relationship. We seriously recommend daily practice of prayer and meditation for others.

GOLDEN NUGGETS

It's Your Personal Journey: Your story is your personal journey, and it is not to be compared to the journey of others. The masses believe that long-distance love doesn't stand a chance at survival. As a matter of fact, many people told us that we were wasting our time. They said, "Good luck with that... it'll never work." Yet, here we stand! You must know that your relationship experience is strategically designed by God to be idiosyncratic in nature. In other words, it is a journey that only you, your mate, and your Creator will understand. It is uniquely YOURS. Own it, embrace it, live it, and love it!

Honesty is Key: There's an age-old adage that states, "Honesty is the best policy," this also reigns true when we are facing the man or woman in the mirror. We must be totally honest with ourselves and our partners about what we truly desire. We must accurately count up the cost before we pursue courtship. Many believe they are ready for long-distance love at the onset of a relationship because of superficial reasons, like physical attraction or loneliness. When the rubber meets the road, they quickly realize that they are not fully up for the task; they see the commitment as too much work. We owe it to ourselves and any potential partner to simply be upfront and honest about our desires and the overall trajectory of the relationship long-term. Are we dating just to date? Are we exploring our relationship options? Or are we dating with the intent of marriage? This is really important because both partners must share that same desires in order for the relationship to flourish long-term.

Effectively Managing Work-Life-Balance: The phenomenon of work-life-balance is essential to all healthy relationships. If relationships were a salad, balance would be the super greens, the core ingredient necessary for substance! It is the essential ingredient that causes relationships to ultimately thrive. The lack of balance is one of the most common practices that often leads to severe stress, fatigue, and burn-out. This negative pattern oftentimes grips us and propels us into a downward spiral that ultimately sabotages intimate partner relationships and our overall quality of life. The antidote to poor balance is to stop, recalibrate ourselves, and assess personal fatigue. If we come to learn that poor work-life-balance is the prominent issue, we must respond. The first step is to take action immediately and seek out supportive resources (i.e. reduce the things on your plate, take a day off from work, ask for help in an area of struggle, etc.). Self-assessment is key!

WHAT WE KNOW FOR SURE

We know that if we routinely commit to choose faith over fear, it works every time! To all the "hopeless romantics," keep the faith! Romance is still alive and well. Affairs of the heart work according to OUR actions and OUR faith. Remember, we must be willing to fight for true love and the happiness we desire. NO PAIN, NO GAIN... anything worth having is absolutely worth fighting for. If it means driving or flying thousands of miles, working through conflict, or simply showing our love in more tangible ways; we must do it. Commitment is key! We must make a decision to commit to doing what it takes to create and preserve healthy relationships. We must literally put in the time required to nurture them. We must also be willing to make the necessary changes it takes to nurture the love we created and sustain it. The most important thing is that we demonstrate our dedication to our partner in a meaningful way that he or she can clearly understand.

Understanding is a primary precept required for relational success. It is essential to all healthy intimate partner communication. Understanding is also a universal principle heavily rooted in biblical truth. It is one that we must hide in our hearts and place into our proverbial toolboxes for a lifetime. Let us meditate on this mantra daily, "In all your getting, get wisdom, knowledge, and understanding (Proverbs 4:7 NIV). Godspeed!

Marriage & Ministry: The Allen's

Hello, we are Tyron and Peshon Allen, we have been married nineteen beautiful years and together for twenty-four years. We are here to share our story of Marriage and Ministry, and what it is like to be very active in ministry while maintaining a healthy marriage in the process. In addition, we hope this will help provide guidance, wisdom, and balance while serving in ministry and the many lessons we have learned over the years! We pray and hope to spare you from the many painful mistakes that we made and hope you will also share in the many lessons that we have learned. Here's our story.

We were and are very passionate about serving in ministry and in the ministries that we knew God called us to. Therefore, we did it diligently, and with all of our might and strength. But during that process, we got off course, and we began to forsake not only ourselves, but our marriage and our family, for the sake of ministry; and this beloved is completely out of order and not the will of God! Neglecting your Marriage and family for the sake of ministry is never God's will.

So, with that said, here are the lessons we have learned over the years while being married and serving in ministry. Do not sacrifice your marriage, your children, or your home on the Altar of Ministry! Do not allow yourself to become so active in ministry that you do not have time for your wife, your husband, or your children, and the requirements thereof. Remember, we cannot work ourselves into heaven. Ephesians 2:8-9 (NIV) says,

"For it is by grace you have been saved, through faith—and this is not from yourselves, it is the gift of God. Not by works, so that no one can boast"

As a couple, we had to learn that any time we operate outside of our gift we are not graced to perform, we are operating in our flesh. The flesh can never glorify itself in the presence of GOD. We have learned and want to share with you that it is NOT your job to try to be the savior of every auxiliary ministry in your church! The Body of Christ already has a Savior, and His Name is Jesus Christ.

If we are so busy serving in a ministry that we do not have time to spend with our spouse, we are too busy, and our priorities are out of alignment. When we are so busy serving in ministry, we do not have time to play with or simply pour into your kids, or we don't even have a moment to ourselves, we are wrong, and our priorities are out of alignment, and the devil will use this to begin to attack our Marriage. Why is this? Because we are not spending time with God, ourselves, or our family, and we are not being refreshed in the Presence of the Lord, but

we are trying to continuously pour out of an empty vessel. This was us, and we saw that we desperately needed God, and we needed to change. This is what we experienced and decided to do differently to help our Marriage, and we pray you will, too, if you find yourself in this same situation.

First, you should never feel guilty or pressured, where you feel you have to choose between your family and ministry. All things must be in balance, and you and your spouse have to be on one accord and in agreement with where you will serve and how long. Remember, your First serving starts at home! Never sacrifice your Marriage or your family on the Altar of Ministry. If you do, you will be broken and depleted, and your Marriage and your home life will suffer; and it will be completely you and your spouse's fault. This is what happened to us, and it was only by the grace of God that we were able to heal and recover from this.

There must be boundaries set in place, and together, we had to set them. We decided to spend an entire weekend to ourselves every month, if possible, just to spend time together as a family. This blessed us and gave us time to get refreshed and enjoy each other and our family. If you do not make time for you and your spouse, you will eventually run out of gas and be forced to pull over and stop! We also decided not to attend every Saturday event at the church. We were dedicated to spending some much-needed time with our children by taking them to the park, seeing a movie, or just hanging out with them at home. We saw immediate results in the overall joy and happiness of our children! Their little love tanks were being filled up, with the love and attention of their parents, and they had our undivided attention!

We avoided the trap of allowing others to stroke our egos to do even more in the ministry, when we were already stretched to capacity. For example, it was important to abstain from being swayed when we were told "that we had the talent to do so," because we noticed this would cause us to abandon our post in the family, and we just couldn't allow this to happen again.

How did we do this? We learned how to say, "No!" It's essential to protect your

Marriage and not overextend yourself while serving in ministry. We learned to stop putting so much stress on our Marriage, and it healed us, and we were more at peace. And as a result of this, it made serving in ministry more enjoyable and not exhausting or resentful.

We were always mindful that God doesn't want us to neglect the roles He has given us. The husband is responsible for protecting and providing for the family unit. The wife is responsible for keeping the home, as the Bible says she is the Keeper of the Home. We are working together to reach the common goal of caring for our family. It's vital to not forget that these are only roles that you can fulfill in your family. We are reminded that 1Timothy 5:8 reads,

"But if any provide not for his own, and especially for those of his own house, he hath denied the faith, and is worse than an infidel" (KJV).

While we were busy working on things outside the home, we still had to finish the work at home. In many churches, we find a disparity in the numbers of members versus the number of volunteers helping or performing the work of the ministry. You will always find someone attempting to get others to assist in the works of the ministry, as they should. However, as the

family unit, don't feel pressured to always be available because someone else believes you are a good fit for that area of ministry. Remember, the word, "NO," is an anointed word. Ask yourself, is it going to overload my Marriage? Don't wear yourself thin trying to serve in every ministry within your church. We have learned to keep this before us, that we are the church, and it's ok to serve in ministry, but not to the detriment of our Marriage or our Family.

COUPLES IN MINISTRY

As couples, we can agree to enter into the work of the ministry, but we must also be prepared when it is necessary to momentarily disengage and reengage at a later time. This allowed us and will allow you time to focus on immediate priorities within your household and family. Taking this approach will help to maintain a healthy balance between family and ministry and not allow serving in ministry to override your Marriage or family. This is a constant call to action that, as married couples, we must be consistent in Grace to minister-The gifts and calling of GOD are issued to all. It is imperative that we consider God our Father, and what He wants us to pursue. Bottom line up front, ask and seek God and listen for an answer before you attempt to join yourselves into works of ministry that you have not been graced to provide or that will wear you out! We have learned, do not allow anyone to pump up your ego, and have you spending all your time preparing for ministry events that God has not graced you to perform. You will find yourself feeling drained and tired while your family feels neglected. Over time, these actions will completely destroy the family unit and produce lasting psychological scars on your family members and lost time that you can never get back.

We have learned to always walk in agreement, be on one accord, and we will never again sacrifice our Marriage on the Altar of ministry, for this is not the will of God. Our Marriage and our family is our first ministry and our first priority. We pray that this has blessed you and helped to shine wisdom in Marriage & Ministry.

MONEY STYLES: DR. WHITE

Dr. Cozette M. White is an acclaimed bestselling author, nationally recognized finance and tax strategist, international speaker, and philanthropist. She inspires individuals to live in purpose, embrace passion, and achieve personal greatness through a balance in work and life.

ACCEPT YOUR SITUATION

The starting point for financial recovery is to stop wallowing in your misery and accept reality. Yes, it is a bummer. Yes, you're likely the victim of somebody else's wrongdoing. Yes, it is devastating. Most important—none of that matters now. What's done, is done, and there is no turning back. Resisting what's already a fact is futile, so don't waste your energy. Accept reality.

Living in the past only makes forward progress more difficult. Instead, accept the setback, let go of it, and commit to forward movement. Not because it is the right thing to do, but because it's the best way to help yourself. As long as you waste your energy wallowing in your misery, you will have that much less energy to dedicate to solving the very real challenges you face to move forward in life. The best defense is a good offense; so get out of defensive mode and get started on the road to recovery with a clear offensive strategy.

IDENTIFY THE PROBLEMS

The next step to overcoming financial disaster is to identify the problem that is causing difficulties. Financial problems are generally an indication of a larger issue and to come up with long term solutions, you have to identify the actual cause of your financial troubles. The idea behind the importance of uncovering the specific problem is to come up with a permanent solution. Just like a leaky tap in your house, placing a bucket below it is a temporary solution. Fix the tap, and the leak will stop permanently. Rather than dwelling on your stress, focus on resolving the problem that's causing your financial problems.

STOP WASTING TIME

Many people respond to stress by using time-wasters to procrastinate. They will dump time and energy into activities that have nothing to do with their problem in order to distract themselves for a little while. The problem with that is it usually makes the problem worse when they face it again.

Stop procrastinating. Focus on the problem at hand. If you're feeling overwhelmed with it at the moment, get real rest so you can attack it with mental focus tomorrow. So, how do you actually "focus on the problem at hand?" The next several strategies will help you do just that.

Let's first look at your money personality. This will assist in telling you about your money habits.

YOUR MONEY PERSONALITY

Are you a big spender, saver, worrier, or avoider? Are your decisions driven by more than one money personality perspective?

THE SAVER

Channel took the quiz, and she's the "saver." The saver is deeply attached to her money. Her hobby is saving money, and she loves to see her bank account grow. She is also known to clip coupons, set budgets, and prioritize financial goals, although she may not be inclined to take on much risk. The saver enjoys keeping her money safe in the bank. She often worries that she may outlive her money and end up in poverty.

The saver also has difficulty spending money on herself and her loved ones, especially on things that are not a necessity. Many savers worry about money and feel that they will never have enough to be secure. Others channel their thrifty tendencies into always. She was looking for a big sale. Getting a bargain makes her feel great, but finding out there was a better deal somewhere else makes her feel terrible. The saver attempts to assert financial control of her life by focusing on details, and she is usually very apprehensive about making mistakes.

THE AVOIDER

My girlfriend, Jennifer, fits the shoes here. She's our "avoider." The avoider would rather do almost anything than to think about her money. She typically handles financial matters at the very last minute, or even late-such as failing to pay bills on time and then owing a late charge premium. She does not like keeping financial records or a budget. She tends to be quite fearful of making a mistake, so it is easier to do nothing.

Most avoiders feel some level of inadequacy when it comes to financial matters. They wish someone else would just take care of it. Money matters can be so complex and confusing, and there can be so many details and decisions to make. It is no wonder they may not prepare well for the future.

THE WORRIER

At one point, Tamara considered herself the saver, but has become a worrier after she started caring for her mom. The worrier has a difficult time dealing with her finances, whether balancing her checkbook, budgeting, paying bills, or investing. She is likely to engage in "robbing Peter to pay Paul" behaviors, all the while self-flagellating for doing so. The worrier continually thinks about money, but rarely takes charge of her finances or strategizes for financial comfort.

The worrier may feel that money is evil and has the power to corrupt. She may believe that having too much money or making a profit on investments means she is being greedy or selling out on her values. Worriers are not inclined to keep tabs on their current spending or invest for the future, and they may alienate their loved ones with their self-righteous attitude toward affluence.

THE BIG SPENDER

I have friends, and I have good genuine friends. Well, my colleague, Cheryl, has friended the credit cards as her besties. The "big spender's" credit cards are her best friends. She often spends money on things she really cannot afford. The big spender hates to limit herself; after all, she works hard for her money, and it makes her feel good to spend it! At the same time, she may feel frustrated that she does not have more.

Big spenders have a hard time budgeting and difficulty delaying gratification in the present to save for the future. The big spender is also prone to fantasies of the financial rescue, and fears of achieving success on her own. While she waits for the miracle person or event that will solve her financial woes, the big spender may spend most of what she has at her disposal, or rack up a hefty amount of debt.

Your Money Personality

Are you a big spender, saver, worrier, or avoider? Are your decisions driven by more than one money personality perspective? Take a few moments to complete the *Money Personality Quiz* on my website. Besides being fun, this quiz with your results will help you better understand your instinctive responses to your financial habits. Please visit our website to take the quiz: www.cozettemwhite.com

Intimacy & Sex:
Gil & Renée Beavers

Gil and Renée have shared thirty-seven years of sex and intimacy. Wait a minute. I thought intimacy was sex, you may say. No, they are not one and the same. For us, one of the mysteries of marriage was not the physical act of sex; it was the development and nurturing of intimacy in our marriage.

While intimacy in our marriage is a gift, intimacy with God is the meaning of our existence. We must never substitute the Creator for the creation. Intimacy with God equips us with the capacity to understand and enjoy intimacy with others. Time with God in prayer, reading, and worship leads to an unshakeable identity. Only our relationship with God can fill our unmet needs. We each have a cavern inside our hearts, and we must not settle for substitutes. We have discovered our deepest fulfillment in our intimacy in God's presence. It's in our intimacy with God that we learn the value of unconditional love, acceptance, and forgiveness. These three elements form our identity, and as we learn how loved we are, we are empowered to love God, ourselves, and then love others.

THE FIRST TIME:

Do you remember the first time you caught your parents kissing and that weird, uncomfortable feeling you got? I am sure most adults can recall that awkward moment when your parents tried to talk to you about the birds and the bees. What is it about the word sex that makes us feel uneasy? Gil and Renée call them a "Childhood of Origin Issues." They are the experiences we live and the stories we tell and are told as we grow and establish our personalities.

Gil and I understand that there are different parenting styles; some parents are very grace-oriented, while others are truth-oriented. Gil grew up in a very grace-oriented home, which gave him lots of freedom with limited boundaries. Children need boundaries; they provide structure and guidance; they produce higher levels of success and purpose in the individual that submits to and embraces its safety. While Gil was not promiscuous, he definitely had fewer sexual inhibitions then me.

The Bible states you will know the truth, and it will set you free. Just like faith without works is dead, truth without grace is rigid and restrictive. My home was truth driven. Those two R's for many years described my disposition. The truth that the Bible is referring to is the truth of God's word. There is a vast difference between the truth of

God's word and the truth many people tell
themselves. Jesus was not welcomed into
Renée's, childhood home or family. Rules and laws
governed the environment.

PERFECTION IS A TRAP:

The desire to gain approval and achieve
perfection thrives in many homes and families
where Jesus and grace have been banned. Fun,
leisure, pleasure, and enjoyment all seem to be a
mirage from my experience and perspective.
Combined with these ingredients, I had low self-
esteem, poor body image, and a minimal sense of
personal value. No, I was not promiscuous; I was
trapped by the fear of failure, causing me to be
emotionally and sexually inhibited. When truth
marries grace, intimacy can be cultivated and
crowd out fear, shame, and insecurity.

IS SEX INTIMACY?

Renee and I brought to our relationship what the other lacked. For many years our differences were our "unspoken" Achilles heel. Until one day, it was not. When we learned the power of being H.O.T. with ourselves and patient with each other, our sexual love life was transformed from an act we engaged in into an experience we could escape within.

Some people confuse sex with intimacy in a relationship. In contrast, sex can happen between strangers quickly, even without a relationship, such as a one-night stand. Intimacy doesn't start until a connection has been established. It is developed over time, and through the process of exposing ourselves and our emotions with trust. Yes, we were sexually active throughout our relationship. Still, our intimacy developed over the years of conversation and listening. Being vulnerable and open about our past and the things we have never shared with anyone else has been the gateway to our intimacy.

Unpacking the Pain of Our Past:

Gil and I have been shaped, marked, and occasionally scarred by events and experiences from our childhood. I have spent many years attempting to recover from and overcome many of my experiences and choices. Gil and I live in the truth that we are a product of our choices, not the negativity we have experienced during our formative years alone.

I remember talking to my Godmother about sex when I was a teenager. I remember her distinctly telling me it wasn't so much what the person did to you as it was how you felt about the individual. As a teenager, I didn't understand what she meant; today as an adult, I comprehend what she so eloquently implied. The physical act of sex was just a matter of going through the motions... It's what makes your relationship with your spouse unlike any other relationship. Sex should make you lower your guard, and it reduces your defenses, and allows your inhibitions to decrease, thereby increasing your intimacy. Sex is intercourse; it's a physical, spiritual, and psychological act that is performed by two individuals. Intimacy is primarily a spiritual, emotional event shared by two individuals that manifest in the physical. While we were able to perform the act of sex without any training whatsoever, intimacy had to be learned and practiced in order to improve our marriage and our connection.

SEX ENHANCER:

Intimacy will enhance sex with our spouses. You may ask yourself, "How do you learn to be intimate with someone?" In the simplest terms, you must first trust and allow yourself to be vulnerable. Intimacy requires trust, vulnerability, and the absence of the fear of rejection. Trust that what you share from your heart and soul will be kept confidential by the one entrusted. Intimacy is for humanity. Within the boundaries of marriage, it increases the bond between each other and the grace in your marriage.

Sex outside the marriage binds you, physically, spiritually, emotionally, and psychologically. This explains why when you have sex outside of marriage, it hinders your ability to see the person you're engaging in the sexual encounter in an objective manner. It makes it extremely difficult to walk away and forget the person with whom you just shared your body and soul. It's one of the most significant ways to fall into the comparison trap. Comparing your spouse with past partners and experiences, can only cause insecurity and a lack of acceptance. Please wait for your turn! You can't compare what you've never experienced. In the book of Genesis, Chapter 1:27-28 (NIV) the Word says, "So God created man in his own image, in the image of God created he him; male and female created he them. And God blessed them, and God said unto them, Be fruitful, and multiply..."

Sex is for marriage for our protection. God puts boundaries around what He values and prioritizes. Sex is a gift from God to marriage. You will never feel the connection to your spouse that you felt with anyone during your time as a single person who you had sexual relations with outside of the bonds of matrimony. This is why the Bible addresses this topic of sex outside of marriage three different times in the book of Song of Solomon 2:7, 3:5, and 8:4.

Intimacy requires mutual respect and love. It is the closeness that one feels for another. It is also bonding with two people as you grow in your understanding and acceptance of that person. As the intimacy grows in the relationship, you will find the connection that you feel with your spouse that cannot be falsified for faked flourishes.

Intimacy must be cultivated by being honest, open, and transparent at a level that makes you feel nervous, not because of exposure, but because of vulnerability. Wow, I shared that sex is a gift from God for marriage. Intimacy is the key that unlocks oneness in marriage and relationships. Intimacy builds strong relationships and deep connections with God, ourselves, our spouses, our children, and our families. Making Love will become a safe place for openness, vulnerability, and a time to give each other the gift of your presence. Intimacy makes sex personal, eternal, and a vehicle to cultivate oneness. Now that we understand the difference between sex and intimacy. Let's unpack some of the obstacles to intimacy.

THE DO NOT'S:

When there is a lack of mutual respect between each other, it will be impossible to create intimacy with each other, which is paramount in understanding how the other person feels. Your ability to see things from their perspective is crucial. We can show respect to someone primarily by how we treat them, and more importantly, how you treat yourself is a good indicator of how you will treat others. If you find it hard to relate to your spouse from a respect and trust perspective, we recommend taking an inward look at your past for events where your trust was violated. You will find that you may still be living through past experiences.

We have to be supportive of those who are being vulnerable with us. Being supportive doesn't mean we can remove barriers and problems from someone who is significant in our life. We can let them know we are there for them and they need us most and have their best interest at heart.

THE CODE OF MARRIAGE

What is the Code? While working with couples over the past fifteen years, we have recognized that most couples have and understand many or most of the elements of the framework. We have identified three crucial factors that make or break relationships. We call them the CODE! It's what binds us together.

TRUST IN MARRIAGE:
GIL & RENÉE BEAVERS

"Trust in the Lord with all your heart and lean not on your own understanding; in all your ways submit to him, and he will make your paths straight." Proverbs 3:5-6
New International Version (NIV)

Sure, many of us have been on a trip and wanted and needed direction, but will we follow the instructions that the guidance provided? Our ability to follow the instructions is directly connected to how well we trust the source of the information we are following. Wow, love is mentioned in the Bible 308 times; the word trust is mentioned only 134 times. However, trust precedes love. You can't love who you don't trust. We are encouraged to trust God and lean, not on our own understanding. How can I learn to lean on God's understanding and not my own? Trust had to be extended and exercised like a muscle. Our first example of learning to trust begins in relationships.

TRUST TRACKER:

I can remember when Gil and I went on our first date, he gave me a time when he would arrive, and promptly he arrived. Each time he told me he would call, he called, this built my trust. There is an element of risk-taking involved in building trust. The amount of risk taken is based on each individual's past experiences. I would have to describe myself as someone who trusts fast and easy; this is a double-edged sword. Gil, on the other hand, is slow to trust. I would describe him as a minimal risk-taker in the virtue of trust. I, on the other hand, am a high-risk taker. I give everything my all. This is neither good nor bad; this is just me. Why is being someone who is easy to trust a double-edged sword? With me, trust is given quickly, so therefore, it is also taken away freely. With Gil, trust is built slowly and over time.

One of his sayings is, "fast and fragile, slow and steady." This is neither good nor bad; this is just Gil. How you choose to trust is more of a personal preference that's based on personality and past experiences. The key element is who and why you trust. Early in our relationship Gil gave me evidence that he was trustworthy by his behavior, his habits, and his patterns. Back to our need for directions on a trip. Let's agree we are each on a journey called relationships and marriage, when we take the risk of following our Creator's instructions. Trust grows, and so does our love and our relationships.

BROKEN TRUST:

What happens when trust is broken? As I mentioned early, I trust easily, so therefore I give-and-take trust freely. One of my most valuable lessons about relationships is people are not God; we are human, flawed, and broken. The Lord explained to me that I should put my trust in Him and not in people. The Bible says lean not on your understanding. In relationships, the trust will be broken; it hurts, and it takes time to rebuild. No, it's not the end of the world or the end of the relationship. In most marriage relationships, time, grace, and empathy are the keys to forgiveness to grow and change; we must take the risk to trust and love again.

Careful with your TRUST

Careful, careful! Your actions are watching you.

They will do just what your words tell them to do.

Careful, careful! Your words tell a story that
your actions don't match.

Which one is the truth, which one will win the
battle, and win the match?

You say you love me, yet you go out of your way to
remind me of what it cost you almost every day.

Would you instead give me money and things?

The truth is, what I need is you,
and that should be free.

Read: 1 John 3:18 (KJV)

Dear children, let us not love with words or speech
but with actions and in truth.

Identity in Marriage: Gil & Renée Beavers

"For by him all things were created, in heaven and on earth, visible and invisible, whether thrones or dominions or rulers or authorities—all things were created through him and for him."

Colossians 1:16 (NKJV)

Why are so many individuals struggling with their identity? I will begin by saying there is nothing new under the sun. The first trick and trap of the enemy was in the garden. Satan attacked Eve's identity. What did he use as bait? The enemy used Eve's appetite to confuse her about her identity. Guess what? The enemy doesn't have any new tricks or traps. If we look at the past and the patterns of others, we can change the course of our future with the wisdom and experience of others. I believe personal experience is a hard teacher when we are people who only learn by experience versus learning by becoming a good listener. We then waste time and opportunities that we can never regain.

SUCCESS AND FAILURE:

In many cases, being an experienced person costs us our credibility. Credibility is hard to rebuild once it is destroyed. Success and failure have a few things in common. They are principles and habits that are believed and practiced consistently? What are the principles and habits that produce success or failure? Let's begin to unpack the root of the epidemic of the identity crisis. Just like Eve, we all have appetites, and we all need to know who we are. When we live our life being led by our appetites, our lives will be filled with failure and regret. When we don't know who we are, we question what we are.

This is what I believe is the root of our present identity crisis epidemic. We don't know who's we are. Our identity is derived from our relationship with our creator, God. If we choose to ignore or abandon that essential relationship with God, then people and things become the source of identity. What is the problem, you say? Doesn't God want us to have relationships, careers, and things? The answer is a resounding, yes! God does not want human relationships, careers, and things, to bind us and become our God.

THE ENOUGHNESS OF GOD:

Identity = Purpose, Mission, Application

The power of Enoughness.

Knowing you are enough is great; but what does that mean? My life verse is Romans 5:8 while we were still in sin Christ Jesus died for me. This verse is my definition of being MORE THAN ENOUGH. No matter what I've done or what I will do. God, loves me to death. No matter what! God's love for me is unconditional. When I first learned of the idea of being enough, it felt good but incomplete. I believe telling someone they are enough without telling them why they're enough is like building a beautiful piece of furniture without first reading the instructions. I believe "Why" must proceed "How". Yes, I am enough, but why am I enough? When I am enough because of what I own or have accomplished, my capacity to experience Enoughness is me centered. I am enough because of who I belong to, not my belongings. When the God of the universe loves you to death, all other applicants need not apply. What is the evidence of Enoughness?

I am more than enough: In Christ Jesus.

I have more than enough: I don't need more stuff.

I know when enough is enough: I know-how and when to say no.

"You Are MORE THAN ENOUGH"

How Will I Know?

How will I know if I am living a life driven by "little" gods and not a "big One" and only God-centered life? Let's do some self-examination. What is the first thing you do in the morning? Matthew 6:33, King James Version (KJV) states, "But seek ye first the kingdom of God and his righteousness, and all these things shall be added unto you." Whatever you do first, is your priority, and your priorities reflect in what you worship. Worship is an expression of our lordship. We become like who and what we worship, and our worship shapes and molds our identity.

Who do you serve?

1 Peter 4:10-11 reads, "As each has received a gift, use it to serve one another, as good stewards of God's varied grace: whoever speaks, as one who

speaks oracles of God; whoever serves, as one who serves by the strength that God supplies—in order that in everything God may be glorified through Jesus Christ. To him belong glory and dominion forever and ever. Amen."

You and I are most like God when we give and serve others. Serving others is not natural. Humans are naturally selfish and self-serving. Helping or serving someone who can repay you is not giving; it's a loan. Real generosity is giving to someone who can never repay you.

HOW DO YOU LOVE?

Matthew 22:37 (NIV) "Jesus replied: 'Love the Lord your God with all your heart and with all your soul and with all your mind.'"

God created love for us. We cannot create love; we can only share love. When you and I love God, we can then, learn to love ourselves and others. Without God, our capacity to love is more like lust. Human lust, like love, demands what it's never willing to give. It's self-centered and self-focused. Love without God is driven by feelings, emotions, and out of control appetites without commitment, trust, or selflessness.

EMPATHY IN MARRIAGE:
GIL & RENÉE BEAVERS

"Share each other's burdens, and in this way, obey the law of Christ. If you think you are too important to help someone, you are only fooling yourself. You are not that important."

Galatians 6:2-3

Empathy is an ability that can be easily overlooked in a marriage because we take the power of our feelings for granted. We start our relationship out by accumulating information about each other. When we are getting to know each other, we inquire (or at least you should) about our likes and dislikes, share our personal history, the good, the bad, and the ugly. We share our experiences, and most importantly, our future hopes and dreams. Unfortunately, we may not spend much time navigating our feelings and exercising the gift of empathy.

As was the case with Renée, my lovely spouse of over thirty years, I was oblivious in how to discern her emotions. While we did spend lots of time talking about the things of life, many years passed before I realized that I could not read or see the emotions she was experiencing.

YOUR PAIN IN MY HEART:

Sympathy can be defined as "feeling sorrow for someone else's misfortune without the emotional connection of feeling what they feel." This was my relationship habit for many years. The way I felt about my feelings was affecting the way I felt about my wife. I was unaware that what I was lacking was an understanding of my emotions. How could I empathize with her, if I didn't know how to understand and manage my own feelings? I believe when I desired to learn to identify my own emotions, I would be empowered to have empathy toward my wife, which would have a positive impact on my marriage and others.

Scripture has a way of opening our eyes to the reality of life, especially when you become aware of something you are not mindful of or applying. There are times when sympathy is appropriate. Before you can really exercise empathy, you must understand the difference between empathy and sympathy.

I love the pure definition of empathy, "The ability to understand and share in the feelings of another." That definition doesn't say wrong, ill, or negative feelings; it just means feelings. This can be happiness, joy, hurt, sorrow, and pain. While sympathy is similar to empathy, the missing element is the desire to share in the feeling with action, not passing on condolences for someone's misfortune. It should be our desire not to just feel bad towards someone. I believe we tend to give sympathy when the situation warrants empathy. Empathy is a choice; it is a conscious decision that you make to come alongside, take action, and share in the experience of the individual in need. Humans are usually conditioned to steer clear of the direction of negative feelings. Empathy empowers us to lean in, listen, and feel.

WHEN YOU NEED EMPATHY SYMPATHY WON'T DO!

If you find that your default response is to react in frustration towards your spouse and not understand what they are going through, you may lack empathy and have low emotional intelligence. This should apply not only to my wife but for others as well. When you think about it in the context of marriage, there should never be a time where your spouse feels alone and misunderstood. We should have a natural response to try to understand our spouse and what they are feeling and support them.

Renée and I have known each other for over half our lives, and sometimes I feel like I'm just starting to understand how she feels about our life experiences. Empathy is the ability to look at our spouse with the eyes of understanding and wanting to know how they feel versus keeping them at arm's length away. I realize that I had to look at my wife as an individual, before I could ever see her as my wife.

SAY WHAT?

"Everyone should be quick to listen, slow to speak, and slow to become angry" (James 1:19). As a spouse, our number one priority in our marriage should be to develop and grow in every area. To build empathy, we must take actionable steps. While there is no magic formula, we can offer a few methods to improve your empathy. One critical skill is to "Listen" first; ask how they feel with a desire to understand and connect with your spouse.

The goal is to Understand

The goal is to become understanding, available, and present. Once Renée felt I comprehended that her emotion was real and her's to feel, this reassured her that she was safe to share. I can only offer what I have. My level of understanding is going to be limited to the experiences I have had.

THE POWER OF EMPATHY:

The following statements are examples of my old relationship vocabulary: Move on! Get over it! Just let it go! No big deal. I don't care. Whatever. By removing those statements from your vocabulary, you are putting yourself in your spouse's position, which will have a significant effect. My level of understanding is going to be limited to the experiences I have had. Don't Look to fix it; try to feel it! Give no advice, no suggestions, or words of wisdom, just your time, laughter, or tears. Remember this is the time just to be near.

Empathy is a great attribute to cultivate in our marriage skill set. We should value it and look for opportunities to put it into action. When our spouses feel that we are making an effort to empathize with them, we communicate to them that we see and feel them and their pain; this is one of the key elements to The Marital Code to Oneness.

The Code Breaker
in Marriage: PRIDE

THE CODE BREAKER IN MARRIAGE – PRIDE: GIL & RENÉE BEAVERS

When we are Prideful, we eventually drift to the island of autonomy. When I think of the word autonomy, I think about "a ton of me." Too much of us is not healthy; it drives people away and keeps people on the outside of our life, our decisions, and our world.

Wow, I am often blown away by strangers' kindness and their willingness to help and even take advice from me without resistance. I am sure most people have people problems. Michelle Obama, Oprah, Beyoncé, you, and I also have this in common. The people you know well and love the most are the individuals that do not value your input or your influence most times. Why?

I believe we confuse popularity with success. Why do we pay strangers hundreds of dollars for insight and information that people we know offer to us freely? Why do we pay people to take us places they have never been themselves? The answer is a familiar foe; it's PRIDE! We don't want our loved ones to know we need help or that we have failed.

News flash, they know! The fear of failure is one of the first signs of PRIDE. We all have strengths and growth areas we need each other to grow. God has given us everything pertaining to life and godliness. Relationships are our most valuable gift. Sure, we have people we respect and admire from afar; healthy relationships require love and time. Listen to the people you can call, touch, and spend time with.

These people will improve your quality of life, your relationships, and save you tons of money. Remember, your strengths are my weakness, and my weaknesses are your strengths. We are stronger together!

Marriage Prayers:
Gil & Renée Beavers

Clean Heart:

Prayer: This is the day that the Lord has made we will rejoice and be glad in it. Lord, please search our hearts and expose anything past or present that has a hold on our life. In Christ Jesus, your life produces freedom and liberty. We desire to care for our mate as You care for us, without conditions and resentment. Forgive us for passing the blame for our poor behavior onto others. We choose to serve and care for our mate in a way that reflects Your glory, and that will be undeniable to the lost and the brokenhearted. Heal our world and restore our families to the Glory of our Father, in Jesus Name, amen.

Trust God:

Prayer: Lord, You are a loving Father and the King of Kings. As much of a contrast as that may seem to be to our human mind, we believe it to be true. We love and trust You with every detail of our life. Today we lay down our Marriages at your feet. Father, Marriage belongs to Your plan to build a strong family, community, and a model to a lost world that You love. We love you, in Jesus' name, amen!

Forgive Us:

Your Word tells us that apart from you, we can do "no-Good" thing. We repent for having tried to live as married couples without your Word as our standard. Forgive us. We confess the sin of pride, rebellion, and ignoring your voice. Heal our marriages, restore the joy of our salvation, and multiply the fruits of the spirit in our lives so that Your Will may be done in the earth. Thank you for your grace and mercy. We love you, in Jesus' name, amen!

LIVE FOR JESUS:

Prayer: To the everlasting God, the King of Kings, the Lord of Lords, with a heart to change and ears to hear, we will follow your daily instruction. Shape and mold us into the people you created us to be. Teach us how to live a life that is Christ-centered, not self-centered. We love you, in Jesus' name, amen!

BLESS OTHERS:

Guide our communication so that we have healthy conversations with everyone. Lead us by your Spirit to use our mouth to bless others and not curse them. Develop our listening skills and increase our desire to serve our mate so that every need will be met without lack and free of wrong attitudes. We love you, in Jesus' name, amen!

STRONGER MARRIAGE:

Prayers: Strong marriages are the foundation for everything, and we make it our priority to grow and blossom. Thank you for the Holy Spirit! We yield to your authority and are thankful to be children of the only true and living God, in Jesus' Name!

SEEK GOD!

Our Prayer: We have a Father that is a rewarder of those that diligently seek Him. So, with that as our reference, let's give God our life, not our words only. Let's chase the Giver of the rewards, not the awards alone. They will pass away. Our Father will not. We will allow the fruits of the spirit to become the sum of our life. We will be a generation that makes a difference by having healthy covenant marriages. Rich Relationships for all the world to see so that they will know us by our love, one for another, in Jesus Name, amen!

Prayer of Salvation: Gil & Renée Beavers

If you declare with your mouth, "Jesus is Lord," and believe in your heart that God raised him from the dead, you will be saved.

Romans 10:9

Marriage is not where we go to get our needs met. That is why we get saved. Salvation rescues us from our personal and eternal hell, and our self-centered, selfish mindset. Marriage is where we learn the deepest level of selflessness and service. Yes, of all the things we are in need of, shelter, love, acceptance, our "uttermost" need is salvation. At the core of our most essential need is a present-day and eternal life with You, Jesus. The Bible reminds us, "For what shall it profit a man, if he shall gain the whole world, and lose his own soul?" (KJV). In a world where everything is at our fingertips in seconds or less, we must not neglect to remember that we are but of vapor. Until we decide to confess with our mouth and believe in our heart that Jesus Christ is our answer to the human condition and our only road to salvation is Jesus, we will miss out on the greatest gift of the human experience, the gift of eternal life with Christ Jesus.

Father, right now we confess with our mouth and believe in our heart that Jesus Christ died on the cross for us and accept this free gift of Your love and grace. We ask that You forgive us and we thank You for accepting us. Today is the first day of our life and our walk with Jesus Christ. The old things have passed away, behold all things are new. In Jesus Name, amen!

If you have never declared JESUS is the Lord of your Life, Pray the Prayer of Salvation now.

PRAYER OF SALVATION

Lord Jesus, I know that I am a sinner, and I ask for you to forgive me. I believe You died for my sins and rose from the dead. I turn from my sins and invite You to come into my heart and life. I want to trust and follow You as my Lord and Savior.

CONGRATULATIONS for the best decision you will ever make in your Life.

About Our Authors
Bishop Geoffrey V. Sr.
& Lady Glenda Dudley

Bishop Geoffrey V. Dudley, Sr., Ph.D., D. Min. Bishop Dudley is the founding pastor of New Life in Christ Church in O'Fallon, IL, where he and First Lady Glenda serve not only their church, but the surrounding Metro East  community. He is releasing his next book, "Familyish: How to Raise a Fabulous Family" this year. It will be connected to his learning management system and podcast on **www.ileadacademy.net** where he is equipping leaders and emerging leaders in all aspects from home, to church, to community, and more importantly, self. iLead in Any Room Podcast can be found there and wherever you listen to podcasts!

www.nlicic.org

Babbie Mason

Babbie Mason, doesn't hesitate to share her knowledge and experience with upcoming music artists and songwriters. For the last twenty-two years, she and her husband, Charles, have hosted their music  conferences and workshops, most recently The Inner Circle, where they mentor and minister, imparting their knowledge to those desiring to enter into the music ministry and business. Although Babbie Mason is known all over the world for her contributions to encouraging words and beautiful music, she remains humble, recognizing her blessings come from above. It is no wonder that Babbie Mason is blessed with so many gifts and talents. She does not hesitate to share her gifts with the world.

When you meet her, you will meet a friend with a love for God and people. Visit our website at www.babbiemasonradio.com

Cedrick & Emem Washington

Cedrick and Emem Washington have a fierce love of God and His people. They are lifetime learners and teachers, and love sharing from their experiences in the hopes of strengthening marriages around them and theirs. Like most marriages,  there have been rough spots; however, they committed to put God first and do whatever is necessary to make their marriage strong. They have realized the importance of having an intentional marriage and the right community around them. Although they have different strengths and gifts, they believe that it is those differences that make them a strong team in marriage and ministry. One of their passions is helping couples live a life of significance and thrive in their God-given gifts while celebrating their spouse's gifts. They desire to continue learning about and living out a Kingdom-focused life in their marriage, in the ministry, and in the marketplace. Learn more at

emem@ememwashington.com

Corey & Tamika Jefferson

Married twenty-one years, Corey and Tamika Jefferson, have tackled the ins and outs of marriage as a team. Christian values and biblical principles are the foundation of their marriage. As parents of two multi-talented children,  the two have developed a partnership that has rendered a long-lasting impact on their children and the community around them. Corey, a Wellness Coordinator/Personal Trainer for thirty years, influences countless individuals not only in physical conditioning but in mental and spiritual wellness as a mentor and confidant. Likewise, Tamika utilizes her passion for healing, faith, and recovery in the healthcare industry as a licensed physical therapist assistant for twenty-four years. Throughout her career, she has followed the biblical principle, "Whatsoever ye do, do it heartily, as to the Lord, and not unto men" Col.3:23 (NIV). Together, they look to service couples both young and seasoned in ways to combat discord and grow unbreakable bonds. www.teamwe.net

Bartees & Dr. Donna Cox

Bartees and Donna Cox's relationship began when they met in high school in Charlotte, North Carolina. They've been married for thirty-six years. Donna and Bartees' relationship's mantra is summed up in one word, commitment.  They base their future together on God's love for them and sustain a relationship that takes perseverance with genuine effort, one day at a time. Together they've withstood a lot and have always found a way to work through challenges and come out stronger through God's favor and guidance. Bartees is an Insurance Examiner. He is part of a team that provides oversight for the National Flood Insurance Program. Bartees is also a retired Air Force veteran with twenty years of service. Dr. Donna Mitchell-Cox grew up singing in the church. She is a Classical Singer, Actress, and Educator who teaches students from elementary to singers pursuing terminal degrees and aspiring vocalist of varying genres www.heathyfamilies7.com

Marcus & Zion Martin

Marcus is originally from Ohio. His military career settled him down in Montgomery, Alabama. After the military, he transitioned to a career in Information Technology. Zion is  originally from Birmingham, Alabama. She has worked in the Banking industry for over seventeen years. Before their paths crossed, Marcus and Zion had experienced both Marriage and Divorce. They also both had two children prior to their union. One day Zion decided to ignite her love for the dance of Chicago Style, Steppin, so she headed to Montgomery to practice. Marcus also decided to seek a new hobby and learn the dance. When they met, neither of them knew how much their lives would intermingle. A dance that consisted of no words, but requiring body language communication, started a friendship. A friendship with two people willing to allow God to lead their lives, helped them realize the two were destined to become one. www.marcusandzion.com

Thaddeus & Amanda Randolph

Thaddeus and Amanda Randolph, retired U.S. Army veterans have experienced the highs and lows of marriage and lived through years of separation due to military deployments or assignments. Their Christian  faith is the foundation for their thirty-four-year marriage. This loving couple is the proud parents of two sons. Thaddeus has a Master of Arts in Pastoral Counseling and currently serves as Ministry Director at Strong Tower Church in Fredericksburg, VA. As a mentor, he coaches incarcerated men and teaches valuable life skills to practice upon release from prison. Mentoring teens in the Fredericksburg community is his passion. Amanda has a Master of Arts in Human Services with a Marriage and Family focus. She currently serves as the Marriage Mentor Coordinator at Strong Tower Church, overseeing a team of six Marriage Mentor Couples. Thaddeus and Amanda are certified Prepare/Enrich facilitators who enjoy helping couples build stronger, healthier marriages.

www.totalgracesolutions.com

Edmund & Iris Garcia

Edmund and Iris Garcia have conquered fourteen years of unification by way of marriage. They have persevered through cultural backgrounds, unfamiliar traditions, and grown in grace. Both Edmund and Iris have served over ten years in the ministry at Greater Works Ministries, located in Pearland, Texas. God truly is their foundation. Edmund Garcia is a first-generation born in the US from Honduras and is a well-respected pastor, husband, retired veteran, and friend. Awarded the top banker in Houston in 2013 and 2014, he has mastered the art of financial education and has become a well-known advocate for veterans. Iris Garcia is one of the first to succeed in her family in marriage; she is a determined entrepreneur, having established her administrative firm for over ten years. Iris brings a wealth of experience supporting White House and Pentagon officials. She is a wife, mother, pastor, and dedicated friend. Join us at www.unityloveus.com

Frank & Daphne Evans

Frank III, and Daphne, M. Evans have been married for thirty-four years. Understanding that God, patience, love, and acceptance have been the basis for their entire marriage, they stand in unison to show the pos-

sibilities in a relationship. Because they have always given each other the space to grow and bloom individually, they have always managed to blossom as a couple. While there are parts of their personalities that are so similar that you cannot tell which one is which, there are parts that are so dissimilar that one would wonder how they really pull it all off. But, no matter which part shows up, they have always executed the powerful presence of love, the absolute implementation of responsibility, and the dedication to each other and their family. Frank, a mortgage professional, and Daphne, an entrepreneur, live in Las Vegas, NV, with their daughter, Cheyenne, and their son, Frank Evans IV. www.daphnemevans.com

Dave & Sherrae Lachhu

Dave and Sherrae Lachhu met online eleven years ago and married 3 years later. Dave grew up in Georgetown, Guyana, while Sherrae grew up in Pittsburgh, PA. Dave received his BS in Business Management and has  twenty years of experience in the hospitality industry. Sherrae received her MA in Marriage and Family. They live in Belmont, a suburb of Charlotte, NC. Dave and Sherrae opened an online therapy practice in early 2020 and plan to offer coaching services by mid-2020. They have a blended family with Dave's biological children, ages twenty-eight, twenty-six, and seventeen. Dave and Sherrae love hanging out with one another, enjoying good food, listening to music, traveling, and binging on movies. They value their relationship with God, family, and building a legacy together. Most importantly, they've learned to use both learned skills and personal experiences, positive and negative, to help other couples experiencing challenges. Visit us: www.love-acceptance.com.

Edward & Denise Johnson

Edward Harmon Johnson and Denise Beasley Reese have been married forty-three years and love spending time with their two daughters and their families. Their three grandsons and granddaughter are their joy, and they all love to attend home football games at Baylor University where their daughters are alumni. Edward played football at SMU in Dallas and The Detroit Wheels. He retired from the Auto Industry after 36 1/2 years in 2015. Denise is a genealogist and the family historian. She has helped dozens of people complete their family trees and has helped several authors research their books. She retired from a Detroit energy company as its first black business office manager in Dearborn, Michigan. Denise retired from a large investment company in 2015. Edward and Denise's favorite Bible verse is 1 Corinthians 16:14, "Do everything in love." www.richrelationshipsus.com

Eric & Laverne Witherspoon

Eric & Laverne Witherspoon met while both serving in the United States Army and have been married for twenty-four years. Along their journey, God blessed the couple with four wonderful children. The guiding principles for their

marriage are communication, respect, and trust. Eric is a retired US Army Colonel who continues to serve the federal government as a civilian employee. Laverne is a retired Army Chief Warrant Officer 3 and the CEO of Texas Minority Fashion Week. The couple owns a fashion boutique in San Antonio, Texas, and a personnel transportation business in Hawaii. The couple's goal is to cherish each day together and set the greatest example of love and marriage for their children. They believe if there is no communication, there is no relationship; if there is no respect, there is no love; and if there is no trust, there is no reason to continue. www.elitecoutureboutique.com

Felipe & Dionna Rojas

Felipe and Dionna Rojas, have a strong relationship, which spans over twenty years that has assisted them in always fighting for their marriage. Their love for each other and God is what has brought them  through difficult times early in their relationship. From immigration and cultural differences, to building and blending their unique family. Dionna is a twenty-five-year veteran in the non-profit sector supporting families in need. Felipe is a retired chef of twenty years and the owner of Rojas Professional Services Landscaping Company for the past eight years. Felipe and Dionna have three beautiful children who are in different stages of development, and they are the proud grandparents of a beautiful grandson. Felipe and Dionna believe that sharing their love story with others is a true testament of commitment.

www.rojasliving.com

Paul & Dr. Michele Hoskins

The Hoskins, married for twenty-nine years, reside in San Antonio, Texas, and are the proud parents of twins, Hayley and Hayden. Paul and Michele own two indoor Adventure Parks, provide mentoring, leadership, and educational  services through their non-profit, Grant Us Grace; and have owned five franchise restaurants. The Hoskins are co-workers in God's service, committed to building healthy marriages through group Bible study and mentoring. Paul has worked as an Information Systems Sales Executive for a Fortune 500 company and holds a Bachelor Degree in Marketing from Arizona State University. Paul currently serves on several non-profit boards, enjoys reading, traveling, and exercising. Michele is a retired College Administrator, leadership development trainer, and motivational speaker. Michele is completing a second Doctorate in Christian Ministry from Grand Canyon University, is an SBA non-profit Board Member, teaches college Business classes, and loves to read, dance, cook, and travel. The Hoskins are near completion of their book, Love-That-Works: LoveThatWorkWorks@yahoo.com

Ken & Dr. Derschaun Brown

Both being previously married, Ken and Derschaun discovered that the key to a long-lasting marriage is to lose in love. In life, you are taught to win at any cost. However, in marriage, one can't adopt that philosophy. If only one wins, the relationship loses. Therefore, they have committed to dying to their old thoughts and philosophies for their marriage. Ken and Derschaun have been married for four years and have four sons. Ken is an entrepreneur and highly sought after business coach. He was a McDonald's franchisee and retired at forty-three and now helps others build successful businesses. For fifteen years, Derschaun has been the Founder of Helping Individuals Succeed Agency, a non-profit that provides training and resources for children and their families. Together, they share a passion for God and his people and are committed to using their life experiences to help marriages succeed. www.vitalvirtualassistants.com

Ricky & Naomi Higby

Naomi & Ricky Higby, have been married for five years, and together lead their uniquely blended family in every sense of the word. Through many unexpected twists and turns, their goal remains constant, a Christ-  centered marriage and family with their four beautiful children, ages three to twenty-one. In searching for resources specific to their blended family experience, findings were scarce. They prayerfully and serendipitously decided to become that resource for other couples and families who may be searching. Naomi is a born encourager, with a passion for helping women to see the beauty and purpose that lies within. As a speaker and life coach, she hopes to help individuals uncover their God-given purpose, potential, and voice. Ricky is on a mission to eradicate hate and propagate love, respect, and resilience. He is an inspirational speaker using the art of oration to inspire individuals to be the best versions of themselves
beasbuilt.buissnes.site

Warren & Zina Riley

Rev. Warren and Zina Riley have been married for thirty-three years and what they are most proud of is they still like each other and are proud parents of two adult children. Rev. Riley is a licensed and ordained Minister, and both  are certified marriage coaches through Prepare and Enrich. Warren, an Air Force retiree, now works for the Federal Government. Zina works in Management at a Global-consulting firm. Both Warren and Zina have MBAs with a concentration in Leadership and Change Management. Although their credentials are essential, with thirty-three years of marriage, thirty-six years as a couple, forty plus years of friendship, and their covenant to God and each other, all of these life experiences deem them subject matter experts in relationships. Warren and Zina have a bond that keeps them so close together that one cannot fall without the other. Their theme is God's Marriage Design: Two Becoming One, Genesis 2:24-25. www.waz87.com

Johnnie & Chanel Pope

Johnnie & Chanel have been married four years and, in a relationship, approximately ten years. The Popes represent a blended family and are the proud parents of two adult children. After casually meeting on two separate occasions, fate randomly reacquainted  them years later, and fireworks rapidly ignited! Johnnie and Chanel collectively share forty-nine years of combined military expertise. Johnnie is a retired U.S. Air Force Senior Master Sergeant. He passionately served in the areas of Flight Medicine and Nuclear Weaponry for twenty-five years. He currently serves as a Mentor, ordained Elder, and Financial Services Professional. Chanel is a twenty-four-year Veteran and retired Military Officer with combined service in the U.S. Air Force and Army. She is a Doctor of Clinical Psychology and Founding CEO of Sapiente Wellness, a Wellness Consulting Firm. Their philosophy in marriage is to keep God first, to laugh incessantly, and to inspire others by sharing relevant and authentic life experiences. www.sapienteswritersguild.com

Tyron & Peshon Allen

Married nineteen years and together for twenty-five years, Tyron and Peshon Allen, are born again Christians and believe in having God the Father at the Center of their marriage. They have two beautiful, talented children who love the Lord. Tyron and Peshon met at the Pentagon, while both serving in the United States Army. Tyron has been working in Information Technology for twenty-five years to help keep America safe from enemies foreign and domestic. Peshon is very passionate about broadcast journalism, sharing her love for radio journalism to over 2.5 million listeners each week on her podcast, Women in Ministry on the Move, inspiring women from all walks of life to live life to the fullest. Together, they endeavor to be honorable vessels of God, and the scripture that binds their hearts together is, "This is the Lords doing; it is marvelous in our eyes" Psalm 118:23 (KJV). www.goodlovingu.com

Dr. Cozette M. White

Dr. Cozette M. White is an acclaimed bestselling author, nationally recognized finance and tax strategist, international speaker, and philanthropist. White has been coined the "Financial Physician" due to her unparalleled ability to empower her clients to ditch debt and develop a plan to create the kind of wealth that leaves a secure financial legacy. She's able to diagnose negative money stories and provide a cure to transform-limited beliefs to the sky's the limit! White prescribes the right Financial Rx to boost your financial health. Dr. White is the Founder and CEO of My Financial Home Enterprises, a global financial consulting firm providing comprehensive accounting, tax, and financial management services for businesses and individuals. White's advice has been called upon by ABC and FOX television stations. Women of Wealth dubbed White, Wealth Builders Extraordinaire. Dr. White was awarded the Presidents Lifetime Achievement Award by President Barack Obama. Huffington Post names her as Top Female to Watch in 2018. www.cozettemwhite.com

Gil & Renée Beavers

Gil & Renée Beavers, 37 years of friendship & love, is the foundation of their 31-year marriage message. This couple's love for God, their daughter, marriage, and family is their BIG why. Their mission is to empower couples to build, repair,  and restore rich relationships with the application of biblical principles.

The hosts and creators of the Rich Relationships Podcast, mobile app Speak Freely with Gil & Renée. They are marriage mentors and Prepare-Enrich Facilitators & Trainers. This pair are also stewards of the Rich Book Business Coaching & Publishing service. Gil & Renée have been on CBS, NBC, TBN, WATC Atlanta Channel 57, and featured in the Huffington Post, LV Magazine and Making Headline News of Dallas. The evidence is clear Gil & Renée Beavers are spreading the Rich Relationships message around the world. Connect with us today.www.richrelationshipsus.com

The Rich Relationships project is more than a book, podcast, and app. It's a community where couples can go for support, gain new tools, and have healthy accountability. Through Rich Relationships, Renée and Gil have been introducing the world to healthy relationship practices via TV and radio interviews on CBS, NBC, TBN, Atlanta Live, HOT 108 FM, and Blog Talk Radio, and others. Renée has also been featured in Huffington Post and LV & Sheen Magazine. Learn more about Rich Relationships at

www.richrelationshipsus.com

Gil & Renée are available for the following platforms and venues: Conferences, Panel Discussions, Magazine Interviews Television Interviews Radio Interviews Newspaper Interviews For bookings, send your request to richrelationships.us@gmail.com or call our team 404-936-1642

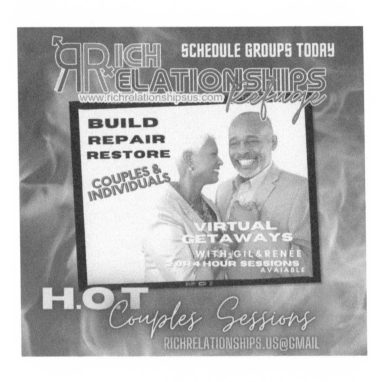

OUR BOOKS

RICH RELATIONSHIPS OUR MARITAL CODE TO ONENESS
Finding Joy In The Journey
Tragedy to Majesty
Freedom from Food
21 Day Journey Cookbook

Available at
amazon

WWW.RICHRELATIONSHIPSUS.COM

Thank You

WWW.RICHRELATIONSHIPSUS.COM

FOR YOUR SUPPORT WE ARE STRONGER TOGETHER!